108182

300.723 BAT / 108182

D1346724

.5

CONTEMPORARY SOCIAL R
General Editor: MARTIN BULMER

10

Data Construction in Social Surveys

CONTEMPORARY SOCIAL RESEARCH SERIES

108182

Data Construction in Social Surveys

NICHOLAS BATESON

GWENT COLLEGE OF HIGHER EDUCATION
LIBRARY
*

531801

ALLT-YR-YN LIBRARY

London
GEORGE ALLEN & UNWIN
Boston   Sydney

© Nicholas Bateson, 1984.
This book is copyright under the Berne Convention. No reproduction
without permission. All rights reserved.

George Allen & Unwin (Publishers) Ltd,
40 Museum Street, London WC1A 1LU, UK

George Allen & Unwin (Publishers) Ltd,
Park Lane, Hemel Hempstead, Herts HP2 4TE, UK

Allen & Unwin, Inc.,
9 Winchester Terrace, Winchester, Mass. 01890, USA

George Allen & Unwin Australia Pty Ltd,
8 Napier Street, North Sydney, NSW 2060, Australia

First published in 1984.

108182

British Library Cataloguing in Publication Data

Bateson, Nicholas
   Data construction in social surveys.—
(Contemporary social research ; 10)
1. Social surveys
I. Title   II. Series
300′.723   HN29
ISBN 0-04-312021-0

Library of Congress Cataloging in Publication data

Bateson, Nicholas.
   Data construction in social surveys.
(Contemporary social research series ; 10)
Bibliography: p.
Includes index.
1. Social surveys.   I. Title.
HN29.B39   1984   301′.0723   84-6279
ISBN 0-04-312021-0
ISBN 0-04-312022-9 (pbk.)

Set in 10/11 point Times by Computape (Pickering) Ltd, North
Yorkshire and printed in Great Britain
by Billing and Sons Ltd, London and Worcester

Contents

Editor's Preface

The structure of the social sciences combines two separate elements, theory and empirical evidence. Both are necessary for successful social understanding; one without the other is barren. The *Contemporary Social Research* series is concerned with the means by which this structure is maintained and kept standing solid and upright, a job performed by the methodology of social research.

The series is intended to provide concise introductions to significant methodological topics. Broadly conceived, research methodology deals with the general grounds for the validity of social science propositions. How do we know what we do know about the social world? More narrowly, it deals with the questions, how do we actually acquire new knowledge about the world in which we live? What are the strategies and techniques by means of which social science data are collected and analysed? The series will seek to answer such questions through the examination of specific areas of methodology.

Why is such a series necessary? There exist many solid, indeed massive, methodology textbooks, which most undergraduates in sociology, psychology and other social sciences acquire familiarity with in the course of their studies. The purpose of this series is different. Its aim is to focus upon specific topics, procedures, methods of analysis and methodological problems to provide a readable introduction to its subject. The intended audience includes the advanced undergraduate, the graduate student, the working social researcher seeking to familiarise himself with new areas, and the non-specialist who wishes to enlarge his knowledge of social research. Research methodology need not be remote and inaccessible. Some prior knowledge of statistics will be useful, but only certain titles in the series will make strong statistical demands upon the reader. The series is concerned above all to demonstrate the general importance and centrality of research methodology to social science.

There are some aspects of social research which are better codified than others – sampling and questionnaire design, for example, are both the subject of a considerable literature. Other aspects – including the subject of this book – are neglected or only treated in passing in available material. *Data Construction in Social Surveys* is particularly welcome because it addresses a major issue in social survey research, the basis on which data are classified and the categories in terms of which data are collected. Writing from a base in OPCS Social Survey Division, Britain's leading large-scale social survey organisation, Nicholas Bateson provides a thoughtful and penetrating overview of this area. What began as a book on coding social survey data is now much more, an overall treatment of the classification process which will become a standard source in the international literature on the subject. In this series it admirably complements Catherine Marsh's *The Survey Method* and Ottar Hellevik's *Introduction to Causal Analysis: Exploring Survey Data by Crosstabulation*. Beyond the area of survey research, the book will also be of value to those interested more generally in social measurement, in problems of data collection in social research and in the construction of social knowledge. It is a landmark in the methodological literature.

MARTIN BULMER
London School of
Economics and Political Science

Author's Preface

Let the buyer beware. This book aims to occupy a level relatively untenanted in the social survey literature, somewhere between the ground in which the industrious practical researcher grubs and the heavens where many an academic social scientist dwells. Its topic is the theory, and the need for such a theory, of a part of the social survey method. Hence, by comparison with some of the classic method-ological writings in social science that have used the title 'Theory and methods of . . .' – Coombs (1953) on social measurement, Torgerson (1958) on scaling, Galtung (1967) on social research – , this book tackles the *theory* of the method but not the *methods* of the method. It does not offer the advice in matters of detail that a novice survey researcher might be looking for, nor does it use the social survey as a launching pad for a general philosophical disquisition. At this middle level one hopes to be in touch with day-to-day practice yet able to take a synoptic view, bringing to bear on the topic of one's choice findings and ideas from related disciplines and avoiding two kinds of narrow-ness – the narrowness of the practitioner, who must rush from project to project and never has time to stand back and look at the enterprise as a whole, and the narrowness of so much modern PhD-dominated academic social science, where the curriculum and the departmental divisions seem to dictate ever more constricting boundaries of thought.

The book also tries to take a position somewhere between the traditional approach to social science and the approach which, often in the name of 'anti-positivism', has called for a rejection of that tradi-tion. After its great successes in the nineteenth century social science has failed to make an equivalent advance in the twentieth century. It is right, then, to question its assumptions and to look again at the conventional methods. But its modern critics, while throwing open the windows and letting fresh air and fresh ideas into the positivist fug, have in some cases encouraged a general despair with the lack of progress in social science – a kind of *fin de siècle* (if in the 1980s one may yet call it that) world weariness, an inclination to give up the whole enterprise and to return to 'social studies', formalised gossip about society. The relative lack of progress made in social science in this century should no more be grounds for abandoning it – or inventing reasons why it cannot be done – than was the relative failure of natural science to advance in the two millennia that separated Aristotle from Galileo.

The best exponents of social science have been driven by a sense of its importance and its potentialities. Social science today badly needs an injection of the kind of vigour and intellectual daring that Kurt Lewin and Paul Lazarsfeld carried with them from Nazi Europe to the USA in the 1930s. They brought a sense of being pioneers in a vitally important endeavour, and they proved able to communicate their intellectual excitement and social concern to a generation of students whose own intellectual and social backgrounds lacked almost any point of similarity with their own. The nature of their impact is illustrated well in an anecdote told by Cartwright, himself one of Lewin's most devoted students, about a visit he received from Lewin

> late one night just shortly before his death, when he came to my house in a state of great excitement to tell me that he had just had a brilliant insight which made him see, as he put it, that 'Freud was wrong and Marx was right.' And he was almost euphoric when he said that this meant that he would have to make a fundamental revision in his entire theoretical approach. I still remember how surprised I was that anyone could be so pleased upon discovering a basic flaw in his own work. (Cartwright, 1978: 179)

The ideas in this book have been aired and discussed over the years with colleagues at the Office of Population Censuses and Surveys, London (OPCS). In particular I must mention Douglas Stuart, who started me on this path, Erica Astbury, whose unfailing encouragement has kept me moving along it, and Edward Hayman, in discussion with whom many of the thoughts in Chapters 5, 6 and 7 originated. Martin Bulmer, a most patient editor, and Catherine Marsh made very useful critiques of the manuscript. The staff of the OPCS Library provided a most helpful service. Finally, I am conscious of a longer-term intellectual debt to John Thibaut and Peter Gumpert with whom I worked closely in the early 1960s. None of the people mentioned above, nor the OPCS, can be held responsible for the views expressed, or faults remaining, in this volume.

NICHOLAS BATESON

To Val

Part One

The Quality of Survey Data

1

Introduction

In the last half-century there has been a shift in the definition of a 'social survey'. In 1935 Wells defined it as 'a fact finding study, dealing chiefly with working class poverty and with the nature and problems of the community' (Wells, 1935: 13). Platt (1972: 77) quoted the Wells definition but herself called it 'a technique of data collection, that is the systematic and structured questioning, either by interview or by questionnaire, of a relatively large number of respondents'. For Wells what made a survey 'social' was its subject-matter: a survey was an overview *of* society, with method not precisely defined. For Platt, and I believe for most contemporary social researchers, a survey is an overview obtained by going *to* society, with subject-matter not specified. Experience has shown that the social survey method can be usefully applied to a very wide range of subject-matter. But if the subject-matter has been getting broader, the method itself has been getting narrower: a social survey is not just any 'fact finding study' as it was for Wells but a 'systematic and structured questioning ... of a relatively large number' of members of society. (The 'social' nature of social surveys is a topic I shall be returning to in Chapter 3.)

Within the compass of Platt's definition we may include public-opinion polling and consumer research conducted by market research organisations working on behalf of commercial sponsors, the investigation of people's circumstances and opinions carried out for central and local government (the Census of Population being the best-known example), and a variety of studies undertaken by, or for, university social science departments. It is investigations of these kinds that I shall be referring to as surveys throughout this book. But it is important to bear in mind that the definition must also include a national referendum or the balloting of members of a particular organisation about a policy issue (single-question surveys), an election even (in which the question is implied rather than stated) and almost any kind of form-filling. These are all forms of systematic questioning of large numbers of people, and the ideas developed in this book are intended to apply as much to them as to what are more conventionally thought of as social surveys.

If we consider only the more obvious first group (and it is this group which will be the focus of attention in this book) it must be clear what a prevalent and increasingly pervasive phenomenon the social survey has become. Scarcely a day goes by without the results of a survey being highlighted in the press or without a call being made for a certain policy to be instituted because 'surveys show' that people want it. Almost any trivial fact can be given an aura of importance if it can be preceded by the words 'A survey has found that ... '. Surveys today are big business. According to Field (1979: 11), writing about the USA, 'approximately $1 billion was spent last year in this country on survey research that utilized the questionnaire method'. And that was not a census year. The 1980 US Census of Population alone cost as much. Comparable figures for Britain are £85 million as the value of survey research commissioned in 1979 (Marsh, 1982) and £50 million as the cost of the 1981 Census. (Both census costs are based on contemporary press reports.)

The intrusion of questionnaires and interviewers into the lives of individuals is nothing new. As long ago as 1893 T. H. Huxley wrote with nostalgia of 'the pre-Boswellian epoch, when the germ of the photographer lay in the womb of the distant future, and the interviewer who pervades our age was an unforeseen, indeed unimaginable, birth of time' (Huxley, 1893: 1–2). Today, however, it is not only the public figures like Huxley who are besieged but the 'relatively large numbers' of people referred to by Platt. Society itself is the target. The second half of the twentieth century has seen the invasion of public life by the social survey.

It is fashionable for politicians and leader writers to thunder, 'Are the public getting their money's worth?' – a question which is almost never asked except by those who are already convinced that the answer is 'No'. My aim in this book is not to ask, nor to attempt to answer, this sort of rhetorical question but to confine myself to a much more limited one: if surveys are, as Platt puts it, 'a technique of data collection', how good are survey data? Do they, indeed can they, provide a satisfactory account of the subject-matter they purport to describe?

There seem to be two opposed contemporary positions on the quality of survey data. At one extreme are people who regard, naïvely, any report bedecked with percentages, graphs and tables as necessarily more important and more trustworthy than one that lacks this decoration. And in this camp also must be placed those professional statisticians who regard all data, whatever their provenance, as equally grist to their mill; indeed it sometimes seems that the more sophisticated and critical they are about the way that numbers should be manipulated, the less they inquire into the origins of the very numbers they manipulate. At the other extreme are people who look with cynicism on all social statistics and especially on the results of survey research. Their professional counterpart to the overaccepting statisticians is a school of sociologists who are aware of the problems and limitations of the survey method but feel that these are insuperable – that the researcher, in generating a set of standardised, quantifiable data, must impose so much of his own subjective standpoint on the data as to render them non-objective and valueless as an account of society.

These two positions, I shall maintain in this book, are both wrong. The former, by accepting equally all survey research, encourages bad method – the choice of easy and slipshod and often enticingly cheap techniques rather than those that are more difficult to apply, require more pains to be taken and are often more expensive. The latter, of course, rejects all surveys. So we are given a choice between bad social surveys and no social surveys at all. The truth is that there are good and bad surveys. At every stage in the conduct of a survey the researcher is confronted with the need to take decisions. There is always a right decision – or at least a decision that, in the light of the aims governing the research and the facilities available for it, is best – and there are often several wrong, or less good, alternatives. What the researcher needs is a knowledge of these alternatives and an approach or orientation which will help him in choosing whatever is best for his particular research purposes. Survey research is difficult but it can be done successfully.

The difficulties reside especially in the area that I am calling 'data construction'. I use this term in preference to the conventional 'data collection' or 'data gathering' in order to stress that survey data are not, as their name would indicate, 'givens', waiting to be picked like flowers in a hedgerow. They are made, not found. (Coombs, who perhaps has given more thought than any other writer to the problems of the data of social research – though not specifically to the data of social surveys – moved from talking only of data *collection* in the 1953 formulation of his 'theory of data' to talking increasingly of data *making* in 1964.) The researcher selects a topic for investigation and then frames a question about this topic which gives structure or shape to the answer. In an interview survey additional shaping is given to the answer by the interviewer through the supplementary questions (or 'probes') that she improvises and the comments that she feeds back to the person she is interviewing. If the interviewee gets 'off the point' she will try to bring him back to the subject-matter of the question. If she is recording his answer verbatim she will edit out the throat clearings and the remarks that have nothing to do with the survey ('Is that the milkman I hear?'), and, when her work is finished and the questionnaire is returned to the researcher's office, coders and editors will continue to shape and to prune until the answer is reduced to a symbol standing for category membership – a code. (I use the feminine pronouns here as the best interviewers always seem to be women. All other roles in surveys are occupied equally well by either sex.)

Definite decisions have to be made about each step in the data-construction process. My aim is to provide an analytical account of this process, which, as I shall explain below, I believe has to be seen as one of the two basic processes of the typical survey. The second process is the topic of Davis's *Elementary Survey Analysis*, which begins by telling the reader that, after studying the book, 'you should be able to start with a set of raw figures and end up with a statistical report' (1971: 1). My purpose is to show how, given a problem to which the survey method is relevant, one can end up with a set of figures. (I am deliberately avoiding the use of the word 'raw'. In a sense this book is about how to cook the figures without cooking the books – how to prepare them for statistical use and yet preserve all those nourishing vitamins present in the produce when it first comes in from the garden.) In one process of a survey, therefore, the data have to be constructed; in the other they are analysed and interpreted.

Survey organisations tend, through sheer practical necessity, to divide up the data-construction labour: one person writes the question; another asks it; there may be a third who codes the answer; and, quite possibly, a fourth who edits the code. Perhaps for this reason survey textbooks often treat the different operations performed in data construction as almost independent of each other. Questionnaire design is seen as posing one set of problems and interviewing as posing another. When these two operations are linked, as in the best works on survey interviewing (for example, Cannell and Kahn, 1968; Richardson, Dohrenwend and Klein, 1965), they are dealt with in separation from problems of setting up and applying classification schemes for the answers. These last topics are given a joint treatment in the abundant literature of content analysis but with a focus almost entirely upon the analysis of ready-made verbal material. Berelson (1954) lists seventeen uses of content analysis, only one of which is for application to material generated afresh by the research; content analysis does not link the processing of the verbal material to its medium of production. But for survey purposes such a link is essential. There is a single thread of knowledge-seeking running from the original research purpose to the question as written, the question as asked, the answer received and the way the answer is categorised. The practical operations that hang on this thread must be seen as entirely interdependent. Questions and answers in social surveys need a joint conceptual treatment.

This book makes an attempt at such a treatment. In explaining its purpose let me first state some of the things that it is not. It does not set out to be a 'plain man's guide' or a set of 'handy hints' or 'rules of thumb' for the new practitioner. These abound already and in my view are usually premature. Until we know what we do and why we are doing it we cannot produce a simple list of 'do's and don'ts'. My intention is to discuss some of the points at issue and to offer a perspective.

This is not to be a technical handbook nor a compendium of classification schemes. These exist and have their uses, but they also have their limitations. As a record of the work practices of a particular survey organisation a technical handbook may form an important part of the documentation of its work and a necessary guide to the user of the statistics it produces. It may have a training function within the producing organisation and thus may help to guarantee the uniformity of that organisation's work. But a handbook, especially if it is treated as a set of formulae to be applied mechanically, has two serious limitations. First, it is always likely to be overtaken by events. Practices are changing and, in any scientific field worthy of the name, must change. Some of these reflect the electronic revolution which first invaded the area of tabulation and statistical analysis of data and now has begun to make its way back into the data-construction area – devices such as sound-recording and vision-recording of interviews, interviews via telephone, computer-assisted interviews, computer-assisted coding, machine reading of written marks and characters. Others reflect new thinking about the nature and use of survey data – improvements within the existing level of technology. Either way a handbook is likely to need continual updating. Secondly, a handbook usually presents only one set of procedures – those currently employed in a single organisation (or perhaps a group of related organisations). But different organisations often employ quite different conventions, not necessarily because one is better than another but because they carry out different types of surveys for clients whose needs differ. What the new practitioner needs is not an exact model, which may be quite inappropriate to his circumstances, but a set of principles that he can apply in his own working conditions.

The limitations of a handbook are shared by any published collection of classification schemes. As time marches on and the world changes, a particular classification scheme must be revised to take account of the changes. Furthermore, any one classification scheme may have a very limited research usefulness in the first place. Although this book includes many examples from current survey practice my aim is not to recommend them to other survey workers but rather to use them to illustrate problems that, *mutatis mutandis*, are likely to arise as long as social surveys are carried out. Such problems can be illustrated from classification schemes that are now out of date as well as from contemporary ones.

This book does not report original research. It does not therefore constitute an addition to the already vast literature of empirical findings about the data-construction operations. Rather it offers a framework within which some at least of these findings may be viewed. Nor in such a brief volume is it possible to present a review of this literature. An heroic effort along these lines was the Sudman and Bradburn (1974) attempt at a propositional inventory based on a form of statistical content analysis of response-effect studies published up to about 1970 that were amenable to such treatment. In this book I draw, in a very selective way, upon the literature but also upon my own experiences as a survey researcher and upon the unwritten lore that circulates among those engaged in survey research. To this survey-based material I apply ideas drawn from an entirely different sphere – psychology and linguistics.

My approach to this academic work has been eclectic and utilitarian. I have borrowed those ideas that struck me as relevant and enlightening and have ignored the rest. I conceive of a social survey as a social system consisting of three participants (client, researcher and informant, as will be explained in Chapter 2) engaged in a common task: the production of knowledge. To understand the data-construction process and its problems one must understand the respective roles and functions of these three participants and their mode of interaction. A survey, then, is an applied exercise in small-group psychology. It is also an applied exercise in cognitive psychology in that the knowledge-production task can only be successfully achieved if full account is taken of the different knowledge processes of the client and the informant. Finally, linguistics is also a central discipline for surveys. A survey trades in *meanings*, and meanings are embodied in language; a survey consists of a transfer of meanings between the three participants through the medium of language.

A charge sometimes made against the survey method is that it uses social process to study social process and therefore assumes that it already knows what it purports to be investigating. On closer scrutiny the logical force of this charge dissolves: survey researchers use one type of social process to study another, which gives them the same status as, for instance, ophthalmic surgeons, who use their own eyes to study other people's. We use 'micro' social science to study the production of survey knowledge but it is the 'macro' branches of social science, such as sociology and political economy, that use the knowledge produced in surveys.

My emphasis is to be on the invariant, inescapable features of data construction – those that cannot be by-passed by technology, that must be present whenever and wherever a survey is conducted. Lazarsfeld and his collaborators (Lazarsfeld and Rosenberg, eds, 1955; Lazarsfeld, Pasanella and Rosenberg, eds, 1972), in introducing their volumes on the language of social research, made a distinction between the *technologist*, who is only good at the skills of the moment, and the *methodologist*, who, if properly trained, is able 'to confront new developments in his science', 'to judge their merits', and 'to make a reasoned choice as to what he wants to integrate into his own thinking'. It is these methodological skills that are needed in the area of data construction. This area, unlike that of sampling or statistical analysis of data, is sorely deficient in integrating principles ('more art than science' is the way it is sometimes characterised) and yet, perhaps because the survey has a commercial application, is in a continual state of technological revolutionisation. It seems vital to arrive at standards by which the specific procedures can be evaluated so that it is possible to assess the impact on data quality of a technical change. What is required is a theory of data construction. 'Theory' may seem too ambitious a word for what I am attempting but in my view the time is ripe for the statement of a systematic position against which it should be possible both to compare other positions and to assess the procedures actually employed in any given survey. Perhaps this attempt will encourage others to put forward opposing viewpoints and out of the contending ideas may come methodological advance.

As any field of study moves from the realm of art into the realm of science it tends to need a new set of technical terms. As the book progresses it will become apparent that some of the present terminology of data construction is unsatisfactory, to various degrees and for various reasons, and some new concepts and labels for these concepts will be introduced. I do this very conscious of the stricture of Davis that 'A high degree of "originality" is a bad sign in a methods text because the principles and techniques of research have been well developed by many men over many decades' (1971: 2). My contention quite simply is that the principles of survey data construction have not been well enough developed yet; originality in this field is not necessarily a bad sign.

2

Data Construction: Basic Concepts

The purpose of this chapter is to place data construction within the larger enterprise of the social survey and to introduce some basic concepts. The chapter begins with a discussion of the theory of knowledge implied by the practice of survey research and the definition of validity that flows from this theory. It goes on to look at the main types of data constructed in surveys and to state the defining features of survey data. Next the distinction and the relationship between the processes of data construction and data interpretation are brought out in some detail with a view to throwing more light on the data-construction process and to establishing its right to be treated as a topic in itself. Finally, the chapter asks whether the approach set out so far can apply to all survey data and it points to some special features of the data of opinion surveys and record-keeping surveys.

Survey Knowledge and its Validity

A survey is a means of knowledge production. (I use the word 'production' rather than 'acquisition' for the same reason as I say 'data construction' rather than 'data collection'; the aim in both cases is to stress the active, creative role of the knower.) Its only purpose is to satisfy the needs for knowledge of the person for whom it is done, and it achieves this purpose by drawing upon knowledge already held by large numbers of ordinary people. The question of knowledge, therefore, is central to the survey method. And a book such as this that seeks to investigate the nature of survey data cannot avoid at least a brief confrontation with the theory of knowledge. The difficulty here is that, as with any attempts to 'apply' basic social science, the basic social science is itself not very well grounded: there is more than one candidate for a 'theory of knowledge'. My approach will be to limit myself to what seems to be both reasonable and necessary if an account of the data-construction process is to be given. In so doing I intend to use some of the terms and concepts put forward by Neisser (1976).

The survey method assumes the possibility of people acquiring and conveying to others knowledge of the world – or at least of that part of the world that they encounter, either at first or second hand, in the course of ordinary living. This world contains things and processes that are detectable by the senses but is also a world of thoughts and feelings. Lewin called it the '"life space", . . . i.e. the person and the psychological environment as it exists for him' (1951: 56). The survey method assumes not just that people *can* know the world but that they *do* know it, well enough to succeed in avoiding perpetual collisions with it, and that they pass on their knowledge so that other people share their success. Failures of knowledge and of communication do, of course, occur and survey researchers have to be concerned with them, but they are not the norm. If we ask someone about his world we can expect that, under normal conditions, he will 'tell it as it is'.

A survey begins with a would-be knower, the person for whom the survey is to be carried out, and something that this person wants to know. For the moment let us call the knower and the thing-to-be-known by the traditional names of Subject and Object. Subject and Object both exist. Moreover, they exist independently of each other; prior to the survey each has existed autonomously. It is the decision to take the survey that brings them together. The origin of the survey is the need for knowledge of the Subject. It is this that sets the terms of reference of the directed search for knowledge that a survey is. But the Subject alone, by pure contemplation, cannot generate the knowledge product. It is only through his interaction with the Object that knowledge can be achieved – the item of knowledge contains contributions from both Subject and Object.

Theories of knowledge have tended to vary in the respective weights they have placed on the contributions of the Subject and of the Object to the knowledge product. Many of the disputes within social science also seem to reflect an oscillation between these two poles. Within psychology, for instance, there has been a long-running argument over whether psychological states and processes can best be understood by reference to events internal to the individual or by reference to events outside him. The disputes in this century between introspectionists and behaviourists, between Gestalt psychologists and behaviourists, between idiographic and nomothethic approaches, between advocates of clinical and statistical (actuarial) prediction, and perhaps also the much longer-running dispute about the roles of 'nature' and 'nurture' (heredity and environment) reflect, at least in part, these opposing emphases. In survey data construction one can detect the same issue in the arguments about the relative merits of qualitative and quantitative surveys and, at the level of the individual question, of 'open' and 'closed' questions. The opposed positions that I identified on the worth of surveys – the uncritical accepters and the over-rejectors – seem to reflect respectively an overemphasis on the Object (a feeling that this necessarily must find its way into the knowledge product, however carelessly the survey is conducted) and an overemphasis on the Subject (a feeling that it is his personal contribution that must dominate the knowledge product). In social science generally there seems to have been a swing in emphasis from Object to Subject in the last two decades.

In contemporary cognitive psychology the 'prevailing view', according to Neisser, 'tends to glorify the perceiver, who is said to process, transform, recode, assimilate or generally give shape to what would otherwise be a meaningless chaos' (Neisser, 1976: 9). In opposition to this view Neisser offers that of the late J. J. Gibson who 'proposed a theory of perception in which mental events play no role at all; the perceiver directly picks up the information that the world offers him' (ibid.: 9). The former view, therefore, emphasises the role of the Subject, the latter that of the Object. Neisser sees his task as to reconcile the two, to render them 'coherent with one another and with everyday reality' (see ibid.: 24).

Gibson's theory explains the veridicality of most perception – the fact that usually 'the constructed percept is true to the real object' (ibid.: 18). His theory can also account for individual differences in the perception of the same object. When two perceivers look at the same object but differ in what they see, it is not that one perceives correctly and the other incorrectly but rather that different *perceptual learning* has enabled the two to pick up different parts of the wealth of information afforded by the stimulus. Thus the skilled perceiver 'detects features and higher-order structure to which the naïve viewer is not sensitive' (ibid.: 20). But the occurrence of perceptual learning does require us to direct our attention to the 'cognitive structures internal to the perceiver' (ibid.: 20), which are the focus of interest of the 'information processors', the dominant school of cognitive psychologists.

For Neisser the cognitive structure internal to the perceiver is the 'schema'. This term, much used by British psychologists in the early twentieth century and with roots that go back to Kant, means for Neisser some active array of physiological structures and processes which is modifiable by experience. It is selective, in that it directs activity aimed at obtaining only a part of all the information available from the environment, and it is specific, in that 'information must be of a certain sort if it is to be interpreted coherently' (ibid.: 54–5).

Perception is the interaction of a schema with available information. Neisser stresses that the schema 'picks up' information and does not change it but rather is changed by it. There is a 'perceptual cycle' through which the schema directs perceptual activity and then is itself modified through that activity. Thus 'schemata not only enable us to perceive present events but also to store information about past ones' (ibid.: 62). Hence they are the basis of memory. Although Neisser deals largely with perception, which after all is 'the basic cognitive activity out of which all others must emerge' (ibid.: 9), he stresses that schemata underlie all forms of cognition – not just looking, listening and touching but also such functions as remembering, thinking, speaking and imagining.

A theory of knowledge that lays equal stress on the active role of the Subject and on the reality of the Object is needed if a theoretical treatment of the social survey as a knowledge-production method is to be given. While the active role of the Subject, in selecting and specifying what it is he wants to know, would be generally accepted by both practitioners and methodologists of survey research, the issue of the reality of the Object is argued about – probably more by the methodologists than by the practitioners. It is instructive to compare the approaches taken in two very important publications for survey data construction that, as it happened, appeared within a year of each other: the book by Galtung (1967) and the long chapter by Cannell and Kahn (1968) in the *Handbook of Social Psychology*.

Galtung disposes of the problem of the reality of the Object in the first paragraph of his book, where he writes: 'It is customary to say that the data must have some kind of empirical reference located outside the social scientist himself, and we shall follow this tradition' (Galtung, 1967: 9). He therefore takes his stand on the reality of the Object but justifies it by reference to custom and tradition. One wonders, what if custom should change? Are the remaining 500-odd pages of his book then made obsolete?

Cannell and Kahn do not tackle directly the question of the reality of the Object but they do deal with whether an account of it can be described as 'true'. They write: 'There is no such thing as "true value" in the prevailing metatheory of science: the value of an object in measurement terms is defined by the act of measurement' (Cannell and Kahn, 1968: 532). Presumably a proposition about an object can only be true or false if the Object has a reality, an existence, which is independent of the Subject who is trying to measure it. To deny that it can have a true value, therefore, suggests at least some doubt about the reality of the Object. Cannell and Kahn seem to be lining up on the opposite side of the fence from Galtung. But, like his, their position is half-apologetic, being justified by reference to 'the prevailing meta-theory of science'.

My purpose in picking out these two sentences is not to point to a fundamental difference in approach between Galtung, on the one hand, and Cannell and Kahn on the other. There was no change in the prevailing wind of custom, tradition, or metatheory between 1967 and 1968. What the difference reflects is a certain coyness or indecisiveness about the philosophical basis of their work that can be found among many social scientists and not least among survey researchers. But the indecisiveness that is revealed when the researchers talk about their work is not apparent when they are doing it – at any rate when the best researchers are doing it. They act as though values may be true or false and they strive to secure true ones. They act as though (to amend Cannell and Kahn) the value of an Object is defined not just by the aims of the Subject as implemented in the act of measurement but by the nature of the Object also. A survey researcher who denies the reality of the subject-matter he is investigating is a little like the religious physicist, who expresses his belief in an all-powerful being but never seems to need to include this variable in his equations.

If we are to advance our understanding of the data-construction process it seems to me essential not to waver over the issue of the reality of the Object studied. Lewin pointed out many times (for example, 1951: 134, 156–7, 189–95) that science advances to the extent it attributes existence or reality to what has hitherto not been granted it. Data construction will only be converted from art to science to the extent that we regard the Object of our investigations as real. If this position can be granted we have two sources of contribution to the knowledge product of social surveys, the Subject and the Object; this means that, from a survey viewpoint, the conventional definition of 'validity' in social measurement – that a measure is valid if it measures what it is intended to measure – has to be amended. Validity contains two distinct components: the intention of the Subject and the nature of the Object. A survey measure may reflect both or neither, or it may reflect one but not the other. If it conveys the Subject's intention but fails adequately to represent the Object, it is 'relevant' but 'inaccurate'. If it represents the Object adequately but does so in a way which does not satisfy the knowledge needs of the Subject, it is 'irrelevant' though 'accurate'. A survey measure is only fully satisfactory if it fulfils both conditions.

In survey terms, who is the Subject and what is the Object? Because a social survey tends to be a fairly large-scale and expensive operation there is nearly always a separation of the researcher who undertakes the survey from the person on whose behalf it is performed; the researcher cannot afford to carry out a survey for interest's sake and the sponsor lacks the research resources to carry out his own survey. The relationship of sponsor to researcher is that of a client to a professional, who puts his special expertise at the service of the client. I shall use the word 'client' to refer to the Subject who employs a researcher (usually, of course, a research organisation) to produce knowledge for him. A survey measure, to be 'relevant', must meet the needs for knowledge of the client. The knowledge needs of a client that might be met by a social survey cover a very wide range of possible 'things-to-be-known'. What they have in common is that they have to do with people, their relationships with each other and their products (including things, thoughts, behaviours and institutions). I shall call the Object of surveys the 'social world'. It is this that must be reflected accurately in a satisfactory survey measure.

The basic model of knowledge production in a social survey, then, which points to the two sources of contribution to the knowledge produced by the survey, is: CLIENT – SOCIAL WORLD. If we introduce into the model the means by which this knowledge is produced we have: CLIENT – RESEARCHER – SOCIAL WORLD.

I should make it clear that when I write of the client, the researcher or (later) the informant, I have in mind *functions* that must be performed in the production of survey knowledge and not necessarily any recognisable *individuals*. In practice, the researcher is very likely to be an organisation consisting of many interconnected individuals each responsible for some special task, and the client likewise may very well be a complex of many individuals, or even of many organisations, with different specific needs for knowledge and with their internal chains of communication. By 'client' I mean the knowledge-seeking function that initiates the survey and that may very well be shared between the sponsoring organisation and the research executive or principal in the survey organisation. By 'researcher' I mean the professional knowledge-producing function located in the survey organisation that can, in principle, service the knowledge-seeking needs of any possible client. In this chapter I shall treat the researcher as a single entity but later in the book I shall begin to single out the specific roles of the data-construction personnel employed in the survey organisation – the interviewers, coders and data editors. By 'informant' I shall mean the knowledge-supplying function performed usually by hundreds or thousands of people. For expository purposes it is useful to personify each of these functions.

Two Types of Data Produced in Surveys

Social surveys can be used to produce two very different types of data. One type, produced as a by-product of survey interviews but not what I am going to call 'survey data', is constructed in accordance with the three-part model, CLIENT – RESEARCHER – SOCIAL WORLD, and will be called the data of direct observation. The other type, survey data proper, is the main product of survey interviews and the sole product of postal questionnaires. It is the topic of the rest of this book.

Data of Direct Observation

In an interview survey the interviewer, as a member of the research organisation, may record from direct observation various visible characteristics of the people interviewed such as their sex or their skin colour. If the interview is conducted in the home she may record overall characteristics of the accommodation – for example, whether a house is detached, semi-detached or part of a terrace. Sometimes an interviewer may be given special training to carry out particular kinds of direct observation. In recent surveys carried out by the Office of Population Censuses and Surveys, London (OPCS), interviewers have measured journeys made by pedestrians by walking the routes themselves and recording the time taken (Walker, 1979), and have measured the heights and weights of a sample of the adult population by taking specially designed measuring instruments into people's houses and measuring them on the spot (Bainbridge *et al*, 1979). An extension of this technique is used in surveys of the dental health of the population in which a dentist does an actual dental examination of a sample of people (for example, Todd, Walker and Dodd, 1982). Strictly speaking, the dentist is not a member of the research organisation but for purposes of the survey he has, in effect, been co-opted into the research team and in the terms of our model can be regarded as a part of the researcher. By yet further extension we can include in the term 'researcher' all use of 'official' records in survey research – records such as pay slips, tax-payment forms, rentbooks, insurance policies, leases, bills, receipts. Although these are not compiled by people who have any connection with the survey, they are the products of expert observation of the social world aspects concerned. A pay slip, for example, is a record of the observation of an act of payment (the social world event of interest to the client).

The problems of data construction in the CLIENT – RE-SEARCHER – SOCIAL WORLD model are not specific to social surveys nor even to social science. An applied chemist working for a firm is in essentially the same position as the survey researcher (in his case the model would be, say, FIRM – CHEMIST – NATURAL WORLD). In both cases, an expert working directly on the subject-matter attempts to produce an item of knowledge for someone else that meets the criteria of relevance and accuracy. Direct observation by experts undertaken outside the interview situation is one of the basic 'tools of social science', earning a chapter in Madge's standard British textbook of that title and also receiving chapter-length treatment in the two postwar editions of the US *Handbook of Social Psychology* (Madge, 1953; Heyns and Lippitt, 1954; Weick, 1968). Data constructed through direct observation by the researcher are, however, in no sense the main type of data produced in surveys. There is a literature on the problems and methods of systematic observation and these will not be expounded further in this book.

Data from Informants ('Survey Data')
We now come to the most distinctive feature of knowledge production in surveys – their strength but also the source of many problems: the

use of inexpert informants. What I am going to call *survey data* are based on questions put by the researcher to members of the public about various aspects of the social world. (This restricted definition of survey data conforms to the definition of a social survey given by Platt, 1972, and quoted on p. 3 above). The survey data model, therefore, contains four terms: CLIENT – RESEARCHER – INFORMANT – SOCIAL WORLD. Several basic points need to be established about the nature and role of the informant.

(1) The term 'informant' is used rather than 'interviewee' or 'form-filler' because the task of data construction is essentially no different whether the person gives a person-to-person interview or fills in a form. There are major differences between the quality of data obtained through these different modes of approach to the individual (that is, the problems of achieving relevance and accuracy present themselves in different ways) and these will be discussed in Part Two, but in essence there is no difference between an interrogation conducted in speech and in writing. (There is also no essential difference between data constructed in traditional face-to-face interviews and data constructed in telephone interviews.)

Analysts of the survey method often describe a survey as an interaction between an interviewer and an informant. Indeed, at one time, it was felt that the way in which survey data were most likely to become biased was through the interviewer putting her personal colouration on the informant's report. Today the evidence is that the interviewer is simply one of many related factors affecting the quality of survey data. If the other factors are favourable to the construction of good data there is no reason to fear that a trained interviewer will bias the data. It is more useful to regard a survey as an interaction between a client and an informant. This has the advantage that it can cover surveys that do not use interviewers as well as those that do, but its main advantage is theoretical: by specifying both the knowledge seeker (the client) and the source of knowledge (the informant) it gets closer to the heart of the problem of the production of survey knowledge.

(2) If the generic term 'informant' is better than the more specific 'interviewee' or 'form-filler', the term 'respondent', often used in writing about surveys, is too broad. There are many different forms of responding, of which providing information is only one. The usual task set the person in a survey is to tell the researcher something that he knows and the researcher does not. This may be contrasted with the task of the subject in a typical psychological experiment on verbal memory, in which the subject learns some nonsense syllables and is then required to produce them under standard experimental conditions. The experimental subject is a respondent just as the survey informant is. But the subject does not convey knowledge from himself

to the experimenter. In the case of the informant it is the referent of the words he speaks, the thing denoted by those words, that interests the researcher; in the case of the experimental subject the words he speaks, being nonsense, by definition have no referent, and it is the process of production of the response that interests the experimenter – a process that he calls, perhaps, 'learning' or 'remembering'.

Glock uses the term 'subjects' when the informants are talking about themselves and 'informants' when they are talking about 'other entities with which they are familiar' (1967: 5–6). The essential problems of data construction are the same no matter who or what is being talked about – although again there are likely to be important differences in data quality depending upon the aspect of the social world being inquired about – and for the purposes of this book there is no need to use the two titles.

(3) Survey data are constructed out of a verbal interaction – a question-and-answer sequence. But words can be seen from many aspects, only one of which is of concern to survey researchers. Words may be regarded not as elements of language at all but simply as *sounds* (if spoken), capable of classification according to such aspects as pitch or volume, or as *marks on a page* (if written), classifiable according to size or darkness, say. Even if regarded as *linguistic elements*, the topic field is still very broad. Words can be approached from an etymological, a syntactical, or a semantic standpoint. If, finally, the last of these is taken as the focus there are still several distinguishable types of *meaning*. Leech (1974) lists seven types of meaning, only one of which treats words as evidence of things referred to. This, however, is the aspect of survey answers that interests us – their denotative or, as Leech calls it, their 'conceptual' meaning. The informants' words convey information about the social world.

(4) Survey informants, then, use words to report about features of the social world. Often the topic about which they report is themselves. The researcher's interest, of course, is not in the informant *qua* informant but in the person about whom the informant reports. It is this person who is the sampled element in a sample survey and it is purely coincidental that the best source of information about this element is usually the person himself. We must be quite clear about this dual role. Suppose the researcher wants to know the informant's occupation. He does not want his information to be coloured by the informant's opinion about his occupation. But suppose that he also wants to know whether the informant likes his occupation. This is an opinion about the occupation which the researcher now does not want to be coloured by the informant's opinion about his opinion about his occupation. What is needed is information about the social world, and the role of the informant is to act as a scientific instrument – a sort of 'informascope' through which the researcher can peer. As informant

the person becomes an adjunct of the researcher in the survey data model; as sampled element the person is, of course, part of the social world. Another way of expressing the distinction between the two roles is to use Campbell and Fiske's (1959) separation of 'trait' from 'method' variance. Our aim is to have the trait, not the method, reflected in the data. The informant is, by definition, part of the method and not part of the trait.

(5) Although the informant is an adjunct of the researcher, his role in data construction (with the important partial exception of data constructed in record-keeping surveys, which are dealt with later in this chapter) lacks the distinguishing feature of the researcher – his expertness as an observer of the social world. There is a tradition in social science of the use of expert informants for certain purposes but this is distinct from the survey tradition. Campbell sets the 'anthropological' use of informants selected on the bases of 'informedness and ability to communicate with the social scientist' against the social survey use of informants selected 'for their representativeness' (1954: 339). Survey informants are neither expert observers of the social world at large nor experts on the content of the part of the social world being investigated in their survey. They are, of course, selected precisely because of their knowledge of the social world under study. But their knowledge is not expertise – specialist knowledge – in a survey sense. They have 'everyday knowledge' of the social world sufficient to meet the needs of everyday life, but they lack the specialist or scientific knowledge of the social world required to meet the knowledge needs of the survey client.

(6) Survey data are constructed out of knowledge *previously acquired* by informants. Except in record-keeping surveys (see pp. 30–1 below) the knowledge will have been acquired quite independently of the survey. It is nearly always the product of direct observations made by the informant of the social world; if it were second-hand knowledge, the researcher would probably have done better to select as informant the person who has the information at first hand. The researcher, in dipping into the informant's store of previously won knowledge, experiences some of the same problems as a researcher working from existing documents. The knowledge was compiled to meet needs that have nothing to do with those of the survey client (which means that its relevance is not at all guaranteed) and to meet standards of accuracy that again have nothing to do with those required for the survey.

(7) This previously acquired knowledge, which has been stored in the informant's memory system and which must be retrieved if survey data are to be constructed out of it, must often have a very different character from the knowledge produced by a survey. Not only is it acquired by the informant to meet everyday needs rather than the

specialist or scientific needs of the client, it is also likely to be a by-product of other activities, a result of incidental learning rather than the consciously planned and directed knowledge search that the client initiates when he launches a survey. An informant is not like a courtroom 'expert witness', called to contribute his specialist knowledge in order to cast light on a particular event. Rather he is like the bystander called to give evidence because he happened to be looking on when the event took place.

Comparison of Direct-Observation Data with Survey Data

Whereas direct observation by the researcher produces second-hand knowledge for the client, the survey method produces third-hand knowledge. Other things being equal, the data of direct observation must be better than survey data. Whatever problems there are of communication between researcher and client occur whether the researcher is observing directly or observing through the medium of an informant. The introduction of the inexpert informant as an additional link in the chain of knowledge production between the client and the social world is bound to lead to additional difficulties in achieving relevance and accuracy. The researcher and the client can have as many discussions as they need in order to ensure that their concepts are alike and that they agree in detail on the aims of the survey – discussions in which the researcher may succeed in sharpening, clarifying and refining the client's original conception of his own knowledge needs. But the opportunity for a similar discussion between researcher and informant does not exist. The client's intention for any given question has to be communicated through the wording of that question together with, at most, a brief preamble and one or two notes. It is very hard to guarantee that the client's knowledge needs will be successfully conveyed to, and accepted by, the informant. If relevance of survey data is difficult to achieve, accuracy is equally difficult. The interviewers who carry out direct-observation tasks may be specially selected and then trained until their work reaches a certain standard of skill. But the researcher has very little power to select informants – often the definition of a sampled element more-or-less determines the selection of an informant to report on that element – and very little opportunity to train them once selected. On counts of both relevance and accuracy, then, the data of direct observation win hands down over survey data.

The issue of how best to test data-construction techniques for relevance and accuracy (which together make up *validity*) is discussed in Chapter 3. Suffice it to say for now that even the testing of *reliability* of these techniques – that is, testing their capacity to withstand variation in incidental features of the measuring situation – is very much harder for survey data (obtained via informants) than for the data of direct observation. If one expert member of a research team can observe some aspect of the social world, another can usually do so also. Their observations can be compared and the robustness of the observation method to withstand their 'personal equations' can be assessed. But with survey data it is often the case, especially when opinions and behaviours are the social world aspects under investigation, that only one person has the stored knowledge required – the person whose opinions and behaviour are being studied. In another reliability test the observer might be required to repeat the process of observing the same social world aspect in order to discover whether the passage of time or any other changes in the measuring situation lead him to produce different observations. While any expert observer would be prepared to accept the necessity of such tests, one can hardly expect an inexpert informant to do so. Reliability tests of survey data are carried out despite these problems but the interpretation of their findings is never as clean and conclusive as it can be with reliability tests of direct observation by experts.

If the survey method is, in general, a far less satisfactory method of constructing data for social research than direct observation, why is it so widely used? The answer is that there is, for the price, no other more direct means of observation available. 'Internal', 'subjective' processes (thoughts, feelings, intentions, and so on) make up a large part of a person's 'life space'. These are scarcely accessible at all except through the use of informants. Many human activities also are not in practice observable by a researcher. Galtung (1967: 29–30) makes a useful distinction between 'public' and 'private' variables characterising individuals. He shows that the public variables (that is, those 'where the individual values are known and *known to be known* by others') tend to be 'background variables' such as age, sex, occupation and geographical location. These are, of course, obtainable by direct observation but they may not be particularly useful on their own. It may be that background variables are only really useful when what one might call 'foreground variables' – the 'private' variables essentially only accessible through verbal interaction with individuals – can also be measured.

Data Construction and Data Interpretation

It is now necessary to examine how data construction fits into the total knowledge-production endeavour of a social survey. In so doing, I shall define the data construction function more precisely and show in general terms what are the problems that the researcher confronts when constructing survey data.

It is often said that a survey consists of three chronological phases:

(1) planning, (2) execution, and (3) analysis. This is broadly true, but what are the dividing lines between planning and execution, on the one hand, and between execution and analysis on the other? I have identified the four main elements in the production of survey knowledge – the client, the researcher, the informant and the social world – but I have not yet set these elements in motion and shown how they combine to produce survey knowledge.

The Cycle of Survey Knowledge Production
A survey is a directed search for knowledge, as opposed to some incidental accumulation of knowledge, and it begins and ends in the head of a client. In its simplest form, therefore, the cycle of knowledge production in surveys is CLIENT → SOCIAL WORLD → CLIENT, where the arrows show the direction of movement of the cycle: the client's felt knowledge needs lead him to investigate the social world, and the end result is a new state of knowledge in the client.

But the social world, of course, is not directly investigated by the client. The client's pre-survey knowledge of the social world, which was at least sufficient to show him the gaps in it and to prompt him to fill them, is to be augmented by the informants' knowledge of the social world. The cycle is more properly CLIENT → INFORMANT → CLIENT. This is still inadequate, however. While it specifies the only two sources of knowledge about the social world from which the survey knowledge is produced, it does not explain how a survey actually proceeds. The key role omitted is that of the researcher. The researcher, unlike the client and the informant, is not himself a source of knowledge about the social world, yet it is he who produces, out of the raw material supplied by the informants, the knowledge required to satisfy the needs of the client. The cycle of knowledge production in surveys is actually:

Phase 1 (planning)		Phase 2 (execution)		Phase 3 (analysis)
CLIENT		INFORMANT		CLIENT
WITH	→	WITH	→	WITH
RESEARCHER		RESEARCHER		RESEARCHER

Phase 2 is the phase of data construction, the subject-matter of this book; phases 1 and 3, the beginning and concluding phases of a survey, are the phases of data interpretation. In phase 1 the researcher, working closely with the client, arrives at a design for the survey that will produce knowledge useful to the client – *relevant* knowledge – without placing demands upon the informant that might jeopardise the *accuracy* of this knowledge. In phase 3 the researcher, again working closely with the client, analyses and interprets the data (which now indeed are 'givens' – given by the work at phases 1 and 2) in such a way as to satisfy the client's needs for knowledge while safeguarding the accuracy achieved at phase 2. In phase 2 itself the researcher works closely with the informant to construct accurate data within the terms of relevance laid down in phase 1.

Three Forms of Survey Knowledge

The problem specific to surveys and lying at the heart of the survey method, which the researcher has to solve in his work with client and informant, is that the knowledge required by the client is of an entirely different order from the knowledge that the informants are capable of providing. Both client and informant 'know' the social world but the knowledge that the client has, and seeks to increase by means of the survey, is a specialist, technical, or scientific knowledge of the social world as a whole, whereas the informant's knowledge is of an everyday, intuitive, or commonsense kind and covers only a very small part of this social world. Specialist knowledge, acquired systematically over time, is always more general, more abstract and more comprehensive than the particular, concrete knowledge acquired incidentally and eclectically in the course of ordinary living. This distinction between specialist and everyday knowledge has been a recurring theme for a long time in the philosophy of science and social science literature about the growth of knowledge. In application to surveys, rather than to the growth of knowledge in a single individual, it acquires an especially visible and unignorable form because here the two types of knowing are carried out by two entirely distinct persons who have no direct contact with each other but communicate always through the medium of a researcher. (No other scientific method seems to depend to the same degree as the social survey upon ordinary people as informants.)

Let us call the informant's knowledge of the social world *information* and the client's specialist knowledge of it *expertise*. The task of the survey researcher, then, is to transform information into expertise. The transformation consists of two processes, both of which serve to generalise the knowledge product: an aggregation of many separate items of information into an account of the social world as a whole, and a process of inference by which the conceptual level of the knowledge acquired is raised. (The latter process is also the subject-matter of an extensive social science literature – for example, on the movement from 'indicator' to 'latent construct', or from 'phenotype' to 'genotype').

All surveys extract information from informants and combine the disparate items of information extracted, but clients differ in the degree of generalisation from information to specialist knowledge that they require. Some surveys (often called 'descriptive' or 'sociographic') produce knowledge at a fairly low conceptual level; others (often called 'explanatory' or 'sociological') aim for a much higher level deserving of the name 'theory'.

Data are a transitional form that survey knowledge takes between the information and the specialist level. They are information that has been classified so that it may be aggregated. To this extent, data constitute a generalisation from the information level. However, data are not at a higher conceptual level than information; no process of inference goes into their construction – a point that will be elaborated upon in Chapter 5. Data construction takes the informants' concepts, cleans them of the looseness and fuzziness that characterise everyday knowledge, and refines them into standard forms so that the items of knowledge of the many different survey informants may be combined to present a single picture of the social world for the client.

We have, then, three successive forms in the production of survey knowledge about the social world:

(A) knowledge as INFORMATION, held in the heads of informants and organised in the natural language of everyday life;
(B) knowledge as DATA, constructed by the researcher using the standard measurement operations of the survey method and organised in the form of a classification scheme;
(C) knowledge as EXPERTISE, held in the head of the survey client and organised in the form of summary values on variables and relationships among variables.

The extensive literature on the movement of knowledge from forms A to C and B to C has already been mentioned, but rather little seems to have been written about the movement from A to B – what I am calling data construction – or, indeed, about the relationship between all three forms. Yet an adequate treatment of knowledge production in surveys seems to require that all three forms should be taken into account. For instance, Blalock (1968: 23–4) rightly distinguished between 'a theoretical language in which we do our thinking' (form C in my terms) and 'an operational language involving explicit instructions for classifying or measuring' (my form B), but as he was dealing with the methodology of social science in general, and not with surveys in particular, he was able to omit the language of everyday life in which survey informants do their thinking (form A above).

The Data Matrix

The client conceives of the social world as a totality with some rather general and abstract characteristics. His aim always is to seek simplicity, to find the few main features of this complex total social world that will enable him to understand it, to predict its course of development and perhaps to change it. The informant, by contrast, knows a particular tiny portion of this total social world and knows it in a concrete, practical and detailed way. At phase 1 of the survey knowledge cycle the researcher has to break down the general and abstract social world as conceived by the client into the particular and concrete pieces on which the informants are able to report, and at phase 3 he rebuilds the client's concepts.

What the researcher creates by the end of phase 1 is the design of a matrix for data (Galtung, 1967) down the side of which are listed the cases to be measured and along the top the variates, at least in a provisional version, on which the cases are to be measured. The social world, therefore, is now chopped up into cases and variates. Each variate is capable of taking on two or more values, and measurement is the assignment of a value to a case. The usual practice in a survey is for one informant to provide information on the basis of which one case can be given a value on each of the variates (although it is possible for one informant to provide information on more than one case, or for values on a case to be obtained from the researcher's direct observation or from information obtained from more than one informant). An act of measurement in a survey is the assigning of a case to a value on a variate.

The data matrix is used in this book as an expository device to illuminate the *structure of the individual survey datum* and the issues that arise in the *construction of good data*. Many other writers have used it rather differently to describe the *structure of a data set* and the issues that arise in the *analysis and interpretation* of data. (An alternative approach is to regard each act of measurement as a statement of a proposition about the social world, the case being the subject and the variate the predicate of the proposition.) The term 'variate' is adopted for the headings of the matrix columns on the recommendation of Lazarsfeld (1970). Here, as elsewhere in his writings (for example, Lazarsfeld and Rosenberg, eds, 1955; Lazarsfeld, Pasanella and Rosenberg, eds, 1972), he debated the merits of such rival terms as 'characteristic', 'variable', 'attribute', 'dimension' and 'property', concluding: 'A common term for all these classificatory devices is needed and *variate* is becoming more generally accepted.' He went on to say: 'Whenever we classify a number of units we shall talk of *measurement*. This is a rather broad use of the term, but it leads to no difficulty; if we classify a set of units by a quantitative variate (variable) we have the special case of conventional measurement' (Lazarsfeld, 1970: 66). For the purposes of this book, the variates in the matrix are the measures actually employed for constructing primary data. They do not include the complex variables derived from a combination of immediate survey measures.

Phase 2 in the cycle of survey knowledge production is the phase at which cases are assigned values on the basis of information supplied by informants. It begins when the matrix has been designed and it ends when the applicable cells in the matrix are filled. By the time it finishes, the variates will no longer be provisional in any sense but will be fully specified. At phase 2, then, the design of the data matrix identifies the gaps in knowledge that must be filled by the researcher working with a survey informant. The main task of the researcher in this phase is to ensure that the conditions are met that enable the gaps to be filled accurately. (These conditions and the ways that they can be met are presented and discussed in detail in Part Two.) When entries have been made in all the applicable cells of the matrix, phase 3, the movement from the conceptual level of the informant to that required to meet the client's knowledge needs, can begin.

The informant's encounters with the social world have left him with a store of cognitive material on which the researcher needs to draw. No doubt this material is organised and synthesised through the ordinary memory processes of the human mind. Except in the special circumstances typified by a record-keeping survey, the informant's knowledge product has been formed without any forewarning that a researcher is interested in it. It seems safe to say that there is no reason to expect the informant's information about the case under investigation to be arranged neatly in the category system of variates and values that the researcher has compiled for the data matrix. Just as the client's mode of apprehending the social world had to be analysed at phase 1 of the knowledge cycle into cases, variates and values, so at phase 2 the informant's mode of apprehending one social world case has to be analysed into variates and values. The design of the data matrix, then, becomes the meeting point for client and informant.

Datum and Data

In data construction the focus is on the individual datum, the entry in a single cell of the data matrix, whereas the focus of data interpretation is upon data in the aggregate. Davis, who in my terms deals with data interpretation, says that survey analysis 'treats classifications of individual cases as its raw materials' and that 'when we work with classifications, the individual case "disappears"' (1971: 4). Classification marks the completion of data construction; it is when a case is classified that it becomes a datum. During data construction the emphasis must be upon the individual datum: it can only disappear later if it has held centre stage before. Survey measurement is the assignment of a single value at a time to a single case on a single variate. It takes place datum by datum. The only way to ensure the validity of data is to pay attention to the accuracy and relevance of each separate datum. It is true that the aggregation of data that goes on in the data interpretation process may serve to eliminate some errors but it is too much to assume that all errors made in data construction will be neatly self-cancelling at every level of statistical analysis from the marginal totals down. Yet researchers who can be most rigorous in their use of probability notions in their approach to sampling and statistical analysis of data sometimes show a touching faith in the operation of the 'law of averages' in data construction.

The informant works with the researcher in the construction of the datum but knows nothing of the client's concepts or theories. For his part the client takes no interest in the datum and probably little or none in the individual cases and variates of the data matrix. Certainly, in a sample survey the individual cases are of no interest to the client at all; their only function is as stepping stones towards knowledge of a larger population, and other individual cases drawn according to the same sampling design would serve precisely the same purpose. Likewise, his concern is not with the variates of the matrix but with concepts at a higher level of generality. Data construction is the researcher grappling with the concrete/particular knowledge processes of the informant; data interpretation is the researcher grappling with the abstract/general knowledge processes of the client.

The Autonomy of Data Construction

The cycle of knowledge production in surveys has pointed to the interdependence of the data-construction and data-interpretation phases in a survey and I have stressed throughout that the starting point of a survey is the knowledge needs of a client; it is these knowledge needs which guide the data construction work and establish the criterion of 'relevance' against which the data must be validated. But does this mean that data constructed according to the specifications of client A are only interpretable by client A? There is a school of thought, especially among some contemporary sociologists (I have characterised them earlier as those who overemphasise the contribution of the Subject to the knowledge product), which contends that A's data are so thoroughly impregnated by A's own ideas as to make them uninterpretable by anybody else. This argument seems implausible. It implies an inability for one researcher to communicate with another which, if true, would make science, which above all is a collective endeavour, (and perhaps all social living) impossible. Practice refutes this argument. Scientists do argue about the theoretical interpretation of data and there have been many instances in the history of science of the data of scientist A being used actually to overthrow the ideas with which A constructed his data.

Two practical instances may be cited briefly. Tycho Brahé, born shortly after the death of Copernicus and regarded as the greatest observational astronomer of the pre-telescopic epoch, provides one instance. He compiled exceedingly full and precise maps of the heavenly bodies on the basis of which Kepler, his assistant, was able later to calculate the Laws of Planetary Motion. It seems safe to say that Kepler's theoretical work depended on Tycho's descriptions. Yet Tycho was a resolute opponent of the Copernican system. He accepted the notion that the planets other than the earth go round the sun but regarded the sun as circling a stationary earth at the centre of the universe. As another instance consider the work of Carl Linnaeus and Charles Lyell. Linnaeus and Lyell made contributions to Darwin's theory in many respects comparable to those of Tycho to Kepler's. Linnaeus had produced the standard descriptive catalogues of plants and animals, and Lyell, among much else, the ordering of rock strata according to the proportion of fossils they contained of species still extant. The systems these men introduced have survived, updated, to this day. Evolutionary ideas were already in the air in Linnaeus's time, a hundred years before Darwin, but were firmly rejected by Linnaeus himself. Lyell also rejected evolution. Bernal points out that Lyell, who was Darwin's slightly older contemporary and friend, 'accepting as a logical necessity the fixity of species, could only deduce that a whole new fauna had been created at every geological age and had become extinct in its turn' (Bernal, 1965: 641).

If data construction and data interpretation were inseparable, the failures at the theoretical level of these great descriptive scientists would have vitiated their data and made them useless for Kepler and Darwin. In fact, it was the high quality of the data constructed by these men which permitted the next great theoretical advance.

In social surveys practice and experience also demonstrate that data construction can stand as an activity in itself quite separate from data interpretation. The evidence for this is the rapid growth of 'secondary analysis' of survey data – that is to say, the analysis and interpretation of data by someone other than the client for whom the data were originally constructed. As the practice of secondary analysis has grown, so have the number of survey archives and sociological data banks on which the secondary analyst can draw, and so has the literature about secondary analysis (for example, Hakim, 1982). The extreme case of secondary analysis of surveys is provided by the General Social Survey, conducted in the USA since 1972 and described by Glenn as 'the first sociological survey conducted expressly for secondary analysis' (1978: 522). Beyond the secondary analysis of a single survey there is developing a more comprehensive approach called 'meta-analysis' by Glass (1976) – a systematic, often quantitative, reanalysis of all the relevant studies in a particular topic area. (An early example of this genre is the volume by Sudman and Bradburn, 1974, referred to on p. 8 above.)

Both secondary analysis and meta-analysis are activities carried on quite independently of data construction, and both, if they are to be successful, must be based on two presumptions about the data they endeavour to interpret: that the data should have been accurately constructed (that is, that they should give a good account of the social world) and that the procedures used in the data construction should be fully accessible and comprehensible (the condition of 'transparency' of data that will be discussed more fully in Chapter 3, pp. 63–5 below).

Scope of the Survey Data Model

In the final section of this chapter let us now see whether the survey data model, CLIENT – RESEARCHER – INFORMANT – SOCIAL WORLD, is adequate to cover all data constructed through the assistance of inexpert informants and whether the concepts introduced so far throw light on any of the standard problem areas of survey data. Two such areas will be dealt with here: 'facts' versus 'opinions' and record-keeping surveys.

Facts and Opinions
A typology used by many writers about surveys separates survey data into opinions and facts, and once the distinction has been made the next step is often to say that facts are a legitimate target of the survey researcher while opinions are not. 'Opinion' is a rather vague term and seems to be used in two quite different ways by survey researchers. In one usage it covers all reports given by individuals in response to questions asking them directly about states and processes occurring within them, from attitudes, values and emotions to aches and pains. What these have in common is that the individual within whom they occur is the only person who can directly report on them, so comparison of the person's report with that of another observer is not practicable. As a result there are difficulties in validating opinion data, and these will be discussed in the next chapter. Since it is stretching the ordinary meaning of 'opinion' to expect it to cover the full range of internal states and processes, I shall call the latter the 'internal social world' of individuals and distinguish it from their 'external social world'. There is no problem in applying the survey data model to opinion data of this kind. Although the person is being asked to talk about himself, the difference between the informant and the social world as two elements in the model is quite clearcut. Consider the question, 'Are you happy or unhappy?' Here the person (as inform-ant) serves as reporter upon his own emotional state (the social world).

In its other usage the word 'opinion' can be applied to a survey question asking about any subject-matter at all. Both 'fact' and 'opinion', like 'datum', are words used to describe knowledge; where they differ is in the degree of certainty attributed to the item of knowledge. What I 'know for a fact' I know more securely, more definitely, than what I merely hold as an opinion. (For purposes of this discussion the word 'fact' will be taken to mean a securely held item of knowledge and not, as it is sometimes used, the thing known or Object.) In terms of our simple Subject–Object theory of knowledge, a fact indicates a similar knowledge product formed by different Subjects when they confront the same Object or by the same Subject in successive encounters with an unchanged Object. An opinion is a knowledge product about a particular Object that varies from Subject to Subject or within one Subject on different occasions. What we are dealing with when we distinguish facts from opinions is a continuum rather than a simple dichotomy – a continuum with a universally and unchangingly agreed-upon knowledge product at one end and with a knowledge product that is never the same for two people or for one person at two moments at the other. Clearly most items of knowledge are arrayed somewhere between these two extremes.

From a survey standpoint an item of knowledge may be regarded either as fact or as opinion. To the extent it is regarded as fact it is taken as providing evidence about the Object; to the extent it is regarded as opinion it is taken as providing evidence about the cognitive state of the Subject who holds it. Both approaches are permissible. Which one is taken depends upon the researcher, who is, as always, guided by the needs of the survey client. Facts, as such, are of no interest to a survey client: when something is known with a high degree of certainty it is not the knowledge product of the Subject that is of interest but the *referent of the knowledge product* – the Object on which the informant reports. Opinions, however, may be of interest to a client. When a cognitive product varies from one person to another or within a person over time this may be interesting in itself. The interest now is not in the referent of the cognitive product – the thing about which the person holds an opinion – but in the product itself. The point to be grasped is that the social world on which the informant reports is now the schema, not the stimulus (to use Neisser's terminology). I shall return to the problems of constructing opinion data in Chapter 7 (pp. 129–34).

Record-Keeping Surveys
When detailed knowledge of a succession of activities occurring over a fairly short period of time is required, one method of obtaining it is to persuade the informant to keep a running record of his activities. Examples are day-to-day records of expenditure, of journeys made and of the way in which a person spends his time (a so-called 'time-budget'). Data based on this kind of information form a half-way house between the data of direct observation by the researcher and typical survey data as described above. To the extent that the informant is given some rudimentary instruction in the art of observation and

accepts his role as observer of his own behaviour, he is not merely an adjunct of the researcher but is actively incorporated into the research team. All this should help overcome the main deficiencies of a survey informant – his lack of skill as an observer, the fact that his knowledge is acquired incidentally, the fallibility of human memory.

But these advantages are obtained at a possibly large and almost certainly incalculable cost. A social survey is a highly 'obtrusive' method of measurement (Webb *et al.*, 1966) but its obtrusion usually occurs *after* knowledge of the social world has been stored in the informant's mind. The researcher asks the informant to retrieve this knowledge, quite possibly to reorganise it in some way and then to present it. Whether this intervention by the researcher destroys the informant's knowledge product as an accurate account of the social world is a key question for the survey method. Half of the art of good data construction is to ensure that it does not; the other half is to ensure that what emerges is still relevant to the client's knowledge needs. A record-keeping survey, however, not only affects the *report* of the social world (like any other survey); it also affects the *social world itself* – the activities reported upon. A person who is asked to look at his daily activities in a new way, to keep a record of them and to present the record to a survey researcher is likely as a consequence to modify these activities. How much he may do so and in what ways is not known. The reasons for undertaking a record-keeping survey and the problems involved are discussed by Kemsley (1979) in a review of the work done by himself and his colleagues over a thirty-year period on household expenditure surveys in Britain. The same basic issue may arise in 'panel' surveys to the degree that the informants' behaviour is conditioned by their expectations of the questions they are likely to be asked over a series of interviews. The issue will also arise when we come back to 'opinion' questions in Chapter 7, p. 134.

From the data-construction standpoint record-keeping surveys do not produce data which are different in kind from survey data as defined above. The same sorts of problems are found, even if they are reduced in scope: the informant's 'training' as a researcher is very slight, the listing of expenditures at the end of a day still poses memory difficulties, and so on. These surveys, therefore, will not be treated differently from others in this book. The specific problem of the record-keeping method affecting the social world is a problem of data interpretation, which is not to be covered in this book. Data construction does not deal with decisions as to the sort of social world that is, or that should be, investigated with surveys; it accepts the social world as given and asks only how this world can be best represented as survey data.

3

Validation of Survey Data

'Validity' of survey data has already been defined in Chapter 2: survey data are valid to the extent that they meet the needs for knowledge of the survey client (and hence are 'relevant') and, at the same time, represent the social world (and hence are 'accurate'). This definition can be made more specific if we apply it to the individual datum – the basic unit in data construction. A datum is a cell entry in the data matrix, a value appropriate to a specific sampled case measured on a specific variate. For the datum to be valid the requirement of relevance states that the client's knowledge needs must be served by obtaining a measure of *this* case on *this* variate, and the requirement of accuracy states that, out of the array of possible values on this variate, that one is chosen for entry in the cell which corresponds to the nature of the social world under investigation at the moment of investigation.

It is one thing to define validity and quite another to measure it. In this chapter I shall describe the approach that has traditionally been taken to the validation of survey data, point out its inadequacies, say why the issue is too important to be left unresolved, and suggest a new approach.

Validation of Results

The traditional approach to assessment of the validity of survey data has been to compare the data themselves, the products of the data-construction process, with standard values – values that are regarded as true. It is necessary to point out, however, that this is an *indirect* path to validation. Although our goal is valid data, it is the process by which those data are constructed that we seek to validate. The implicit argument behind all validation of results is that if a certain data-construction process can be shown to produce valid data on one occasion that process is itself validated, which means that data produced by it on other occasions should also be valid. Later in this chapter I shall present the case for a *direct* attempt at the validation of the data-construction process.

According to the traditional approach, the data are regarded as valid to the extent that they match the standard values. In effect, a set of parallel columns is introduced into the data matrix (see Figure 3.1), and a datum for a given case is validated by comparing it with the standard value for that same case.

Case	Variate A		Variate B	
	Datum	Standard	Datum	Standard
1				
2				
3				

Figure 3.1 *Case × variate matrix comparing obtained datum with standard value.*

There are two ways of obtaining a standard value for comparison with a survey datum, one conceptually similar to 'criterion validation', as used in assessing psychological tests, and the other to psychological 'construct validation' (Nunnally, 1967). These will now be discussed in turn.

Validation against an Obtained Criterion Value
The most straightforward way in which to evaluate a datum is to compare it with a value we know to be valid obtained on the same variate for the same case. Although the idea is straightforward, however, the practice of it is difficult to achieve. The value, if it is to serve as a criterion against which we can judge the worth of the survey datum, must be clearly superior to the datum; we must be confident in its validity. But if it is to be superior to the datum it must not be based upon information obtained from inexpert informants, since it is, above all, this feature of survey method that throws survey data into doubt in the first place. The criterion value, therefore, must be based upon direct observation by an expert observer (see Chapter 2, pp. 20–1 above, for some discussion of the superiority of the 'data of direct observation' to 'survey data' proper). But much of the social world is simply not accessible to an expert observer. Almost all states and events internal to the individual can, at the present stage of social science technique, only be reported upon by the individuals within whom they reside. Sudman and Bradburn (1974) and Kalton and Schuman (1982), respectively, describe these as 'in principle' and 'in theory' inaccessible to an observer. I would prefer to be more cautious and to say that at present they are *in practice* not capable of being observed from without. Exactly the same limitation applies to a great many behaviours of the kind inquired about in surveys. Details of an individual's past behaviour are often known only to himself.

Despite these limitations, survey methodologists have shown much ingenuity in devising means of acquiring criterion observations to set against informant-based data. These tend to fall into two types. One is when knowledge is sought about some contemporary state of the external social world which is susceptible to direct observation by the researcher but is more conveniently found out about by asking informants questions. For instance, the informant may be asked about recent purchases of groceries or about the number of rooms in his house. For validational purposes the researcher may then ask actually to see the contents of the pantry or to be given a conducted tour of the dwelling, and from his own observations he can construct criterion values to compare with the survey data proper. The other type of criterion value is obtained from 'official' records. Here the part of the social world under scrutiny is a person's behaviour *vis-à-vis* some official agency which keeps its own records of the interaction and is prepared to release them to the researcher. These records are certainly independent of the informant's own recollections, and since they are kept by people whose job is, in part, to keep such records we can regard them as examples of 'expert' observation. They are far from infallible, however, being kept for administrative rather than research purposes, sometimes lacking important information from a survey viewpoint, and often presenting formidable problems in matching the survey case to the case covered in the records.

The earliest and perhaps still the best-known example of a survey specifically designed to test answers from informants against official records is the Denver Validity Survey conducted in the spring of 1949 in Denver, Colorado, and reported in several articles over many years (for example, Parry and Crossley, 1950; Cahalan, 1968). The topics studied included whether the person was registered to vote, whether he had voted in various national and city elections, whether he possessed a driving licence, a public library card, a car, or a telephone. A similar survey, conducted in Chicago more recently, also obtained information about registration to vote, voting behaviour and possession of a library card (Bradburn, Sudman, *et al.*, 1979: ch. 1). Since its aim was to study the effects of questions about 'threatening' topics, the Chicago study included a sample of recently declared bankrupts and a sample of people who had been charged with drunken driving in the previous year, and these people were asked whether they had had these experiences. Many other checks of data validity against official records can be found reviewed in Cannell and Kahn (1968). Cannell and his colleagues have themselves carried out investigations of the validity of medical data (for example, stays in hospital and visits to the doctor) using hospital discharge, clinic and physician records as the source of criterion values. This work is summarised by Cannell, Marquis and Laurent (1977: 4–17).

No amount of ingenuity can create criterion values for all aspects of the social world. The internal social world is not at present accessible to expert observation. And, of the external world, it is only states existing at the time of the survey that are, even potentially, directly accessible to the researcher in person. For previous states that have differed from the present one he must rely on available records, and these cover only a special subset of the individual's past behaviour – his interactions with officialdom. Furthermore, official records themselves often are based upon information supplied by the individual. For instance, the Denver survey included validational checks on the person's age and whether he owned or rented his home. It seems very likely that the criterion values for these variates were themselves based on information supplied by the person on some previous occasion.

In these circumstances, survey researchers often fall back upon the comparison of survey data (that is, data based on information supplied by inexpert informants) with criterion values that also are merely survey data and that therefore lack the clear superiority of the data of direct observation. Within a survey one informant-based datum may be checked for inconsistency with another. The inconsistency here may be logical (for example, the same person described as aged 18 in one answer and 28 in another) or empirical (for example, a person aged 18 and described as a doctor). It is also possible to make two separate surveys of a set of sampled cases and to compare the results. This is best illustrated by the post-enumeration surveys carried out on a subsample of cases after a national census. These began with a survey following the 1950 Censuses of Population, Housing and Agriculture in the USA and have since then been taken in many countries. Consistency checks within a survey have the advantage that there is almost no elapse of time between the taking of the two measurements, but there is a limit to the amount of these checks that can be made without overburdening or irritating the informant. Repeat surveys can, in theory, provide duplicate values for all the cells in the data matrix but they are plagued by other problems: the researcher has to find the informant again, ensure that exactly the same case is measured on exactly the same variate on both occasions (often difficult, especially if the social world has changed between the two surveys), overcome any failure of memory (that is, changes in the informant's cognitive schema that have occurred since the first survey was taken) and cope with any reluctance that the informant may have to go through the survey process a second time.

The problem with internal consistency checks and repeat surveys like post-enumeration surveys is that the criterion values, being survey data proper, are themselves of doubtful validity. They therefore constitute tests of reliability, the robustness of a measurement method to resist various adventitious changes in its use (such as a change in the person taking the measurement or differences in the location, time or context of an act of measurement), rather than validity. If a datum is compared with a criterion value obtained using the same method and the two are found to agree, it is possible that both are wrong because of some constant deficiency of the method. And if they disagree, while we can be sure that one is wrong, we cannot be certain which is right and which is wrong and there is the possibility that both are wrong. Reliability is a necessary but not a sufficient condition for validity.

This is not to impugn the usefulness of consistency checks and repeat surveys. If we combine the examples given above of logical and empirical consistency checks we have a person aged either 18 or 28 who is described as a doctor. It is possible (if we limit ourselves to this information and accept the rulings in the consistency checks) to conclude either that he is 18 and neither 28 nor a doctor, or that he is a 28-year-old doctor and not 18. Obviously the weight of evidence here – the two pieces of information against one – is in favour of the latter alternative, and this is the type of reasoning used in resolving differences revealed by consistency checks. With a post-enumeration survey the assumption is made that the survey, being carried out by skilled interviewers asking rather detailed questions, is more likely to be valid than the census, which uses self-completion forms and rather simple questions. But a considerable element of doubt remains; the verdict has to be that survey data proper cannot be satisfactorily validated against survey data proper.

Validation against a Predicted Theoretical Value (Construct Validation)

We have now considered two ways of obtaining a criterion value for a cell in the data matrix as a standard against which the constructed datum can be validated. One way obtains a valid criterion but is only applicable to a small part of the phenomena covered in social surveys, while the other applies to all survey phenomena but is not guaranteed to obtain a valid criterion. There is another validational method, used in psychological measurement to evaluate constructs for which no criterion measure exists, which examines the position of the measured construct in a 'nomological network' (Cronbach and Meehl, 1955: 290) – a tissue of relationships between theoretical constructs. To the degree that the measure under study shows the relationships theoretically predicted for it, it is regarded as having 'construct validity'. In this way measures of personality, attitude and opinion, topics that form part of the internal social world in a survey sense and that are therefore inaccessible to direct observation, become capable of being validated.

This approach can also be applied to the validation of survey data. For any survey datum, about either the external or internal social world, we can ask whether it conforms to theoretical expectation. Clearly, if we had a network of well-established theory predicting a value for a particular cell in the data matrix we could regard this value as valid for that cell and therefore as a standard against which to measure an obtained datum. In the current state of social theory, however, this kind of 'point prediction' is not found often enough to be of any practical use. Moreover, it is in the nature of surveys as a descriptive tool that they tend to be used to break new ground, to investigate social phenomena not yet studied, and that therefore they tend to run ahead of theory.

Aggregate values (that is, patterns of data as opposed to an individual datum) may sometimes be theoretically predicted and survey aggregates checked for validity against them. For instance, 'smoothness' is a characteristic that may be expected in theory to be found in many statistical distributions, and Kruskal (1981: 509) has pointed to 'lack of smoothness' as an attribute of aggregated data that may indicate the presence of error. Myers (1954) showed that when ages reported in the US Census were tabulated according to their last digit, two fell markedly above the theoretically expected 'smooth' value of 10 per cent for each digit. This occurred on every census from 1880 to 1950, although to a lesser extent as time went by. The two deviant digits were 0 and 5, which strongly suggested that the ages were being rounded off when reported.

A similar theoretical prediction of valid aggregate values is made when the effects of different data-construction techniques are compared in methodological studies. The theory states that the higher (or lower) the average value obtained, the greater is the validity of the technique used to obtain it. This approach was taken by Fellegi and Sunter in an experimental test they carried out in preparation for the 1971 Canadian Travel Survey. Their dependent variable measures were of trips and travel expenses reported. They write: 'In interpreting the results we assume that unreal trips and expenses are never reported but that some real trips and expenses may not be reported' (Fellegi and Sunter, 1973: 352). The reasoning behind this assumption is that informants will forget to report some trips and expenses and that the best data-construction technique is that one which minimises their forgetfulness. The same reasoning has led other researchers to make the same assumption about measures of consumer expenditure and of sickness episodes. Bradburn, Sudman et al., (1979) made this assumption about answers to questions about topics on which people are likely to be somewhat sensitive, such as their gambling, drinking, drug-taking and sexual behaviour. But the reasoning behind the assumption here was not that informants would forget to report the behaviours so much as that they would feel reluctant to report them, in which case the best technique is that which minimises their reluctance.

While this construct-validation approach provides a useful supplement to the two criterion-validation methods described above, like them it has serious limitations. First, as Kalton and Schuman say about this approach to the validation of responses to non-factual questions, 'At the current stage of theory development in the social sciences, a failure of data to fit a theory is usually as likely to cast doubt on the theory as on the measuring instruments' (1982: 43). Next, it can only serve to validate aggregate values – patterns of data rather than an individual datum. (The criterion-validation methods are often used only to validate at aggregate level, but there the potentiality of validation at the level of the datum exists.) But comparison with a standard value at the aggregate level throws rather little light upon the detailed working of the data-construction technique. If we find a difference between our obtained and predicted aggregate values, we know that something has gone wrong but we do not know which cases have been wrongly measured. Suppose, for instance, 12 per cent of ages end in zero when only 10 per cent are expected to do so. We know that there is error here but we cannot identify the faulty cases. If, on the other hand, we find no difference we cannot conclude that the individual cases have been measured correctly; errors of measurement may simply have cancelled out. Wyner compared the number of times that a sample of former heroin addicts had been arrested in New York City in a given period, according to their own reports, with the number recorded in the police files. He found that the mean number of events agreed (nine, to the nearest whole number) but that 'only 10 out of 79 people in the sample gave completely accurate responses' (Wyner, 1980: 167). Of course, as with any check against official records, the records may have been in error, but if we accept these figures as illustrative they show that agreement between an obtained aggregate and a predicted aggregate may conceal a wealth of invalidity at the level of the individual case.

The argument is sometimes advanced that invalidity at datum level is unimportant; after all, data interpretation deals with aggregates, not with individual data, and so long as the aggregates are valid then the data may be defined as valid. But data may be aggregated in many different ways, and errors that cancel out when marginal totals are calculated may not do so when various internal analyses are performed and subgroups identified. The researcher may know what analyses, and therefore what forms of aggregation, his commissioning client needs but cannot know to what future uses his data may be put by secondary users. The wise data constructor avoids the cavalier assumption that all invalidity will be self-cancelling and has a care to the quality of the individual datum.

Is Validation Necessary?

In view of the difficulty of validating survey results it is not surprising that most surveys attempt very little. Even the best usually attempt nothing at datum level beyond a few simple internal-consistency checks. At data level they may compare their aggregate values with comparable values obtained in other informant-based surveys. A 'continuous' or 'repeated' survey, for example, can always compare its results this time with its results on previous occasions, and an *ad hoc* (one-off) survey can check its results against those obtained on another survey that is generally regarded as setting a standard in this field. It is all too easy to enumerate the limitations of this kind of validation: (1) it works only at aggregate level (a datum-by-datum comparison is not possible); (2) it validates against a standard which itself is based on survey data proper (hence it is a test of reliability rather than validity); (3) it is limited in application to variates which have been measured in a comparable form on other recent surveys; (4) it compares measures taken on one set of cases with measures taken on another (so when, for instance, the comparison is with a set of survey results obtained at an earlier time, a difference may reflect some defect in method, but equally may reflect a change that has actually taken place in the social world).

In the absence of fully satisfactory validational tests, most researchers *assume* the validity of their data. (No doubt some few survey practitioners would take comfort from the fact that their data are so hard to validate because, of course, they are equally hard to invalidate – and this may be one good reason for scepticism about the survey method.) But can validity simply be assumed? In this chapter I have talked about the conceptual and technical problems of validational studies but I have not talked about their results. In my view the usefulness of these results is not proportional to the amount of effort that has been expended in producing them because they have not so far had much success in advancing the theory of data construction in surveys. The main theoretical contribution that has come from this work had been made by Charles Cannell and his colleagues, although their attention has been exclusively upon interviewing (which makes up a part, but not the whole, of the data-construction process). One generalisation that Cannell and Kahn • make, at the beginning of their review of the studies in reliability and validity, is that most of these studies 'report significant invalidity in the data' (1968: 540). They go on to say that, although these studies are published precisely because they reveal invalidity in data, and consequently they may seem to overstate the incidence of invalidity in surveys generally, it is also a fact that only well-constructed data are likely to be made available for validity tests. Even the careful and competent researcher may produce invalid data; validity cannot be taken for granted.

The good researcher would no doubt deny that he does take validity for granted. But, for lack of systematic validational procedures applicable at the level of the individual datum, he falls back upon the surface appearance of his methods and his results – what in psychological measurement is known as 'face validity' (Nunnally, 1967). This amounts to little more than the requirement that common sense should be the yardstick. But the validational studies have shown that an apparently sensible question asked by an apparently sensible interviewer is not guaranteed to obtain an answer that is both relevant and accurate. And if common sense is taken as the criterion for judging data, and hence as being necessarily superior to the obtained data, why bother with a survey at all? Why should not the researcher set up a data matrix and fill in the cell values himself, applying common sense and educated guesswork? This is not an entirely frivolous suggestion; surveys vary in how much care is taken over the construction of the data, and there have been some conducted in which this procedure might well have improved the validity of the data.

Data Validation Needed for the Commissioning Client
A more sophisticated version of the assumption-of-validity argument maintains not that data are valid in any absolute sense but that they are valid enough. At the end of an otherwise excellent article on survey error, Deming (1944) put forward the perhaps rather cynical view that the level of accuracy *needed* in surveys was in fact the level *achieved*, both being below the level *claimed*. At first sight this might seem an attractive argument. Surveys are conducted in order to satisfy the needs for knowledge of the clients who commission them. If the survey data are valid enough to enable those knowledge needs to be satisfied, then survey data pass the quality test. There may be plenty of invalid entries in the data matrix but there are not enough to spoil the pudding. Evidence for this contention is supplied by the sheer proliferation of surveys. The clients keep coming back for more and therefore, it seems, are happy with what they are getting. But the matter cannot be left to rest here. We need to ask how, in the absence of the results of validation tests, the clients judge the quality of the data constructed for them.

According to Noelle-Neumann, who for many years has been urging the survey-research community to be less complacent about the quality of its data, election forecasts have had a decisive effect in demonstrating the adequacy of the survey method. She wrote two decades ago: 'Without such a demonstration there would not now be hundreds of institutions which carry out sample surveys; without this easily comprehensible proof public opinion research would scarcely be taken seriously and shown the current tacit respect in politics, and in economics and cultural life' (Noelle, 1962: 7). But these forecasts, the validity of which anyway is demonstrated only at aggregate level, make up a very small and very unrepresentative part of all survey research (the estimate of Field [1979] is that of the $1,000 million spent on survey research in the USA in 1978 only 2 per cent went on political polling) and do not constitute a sound basis for evaluating all survey data.

Client contentment with the quality of data received seems not to be based on a very firm foundation. But what is the evidence that the quality of data produced now will persist into the future? If we look more closely at the social context in which surveys are produced we shall see that there are pressures leading all the time to a deterioration of survey data.

Surveys, perhaps uniquely among social science methods, have an applied use; indeed, because of their costliness, with the exception of the small number of surveys carried out by academics for themselves almost all their use is applied. (Field [1979] allocates 90 per cent of spending on surveys in 1978 in the USA to market research and the remaining 8 per cent to what he calls 'public policy' surveys.) The survey method is a commodity, sold and bought in the market-place, with firms and research organisations competing to win the favour of commissioning clients. What factors do clients take into account when placing an order for a social survey? Surveys nearly always have a policy function, whether they are in the commercial or the public administration sector; survey evidence is obtained in order to formulate, apply, or appraise a policy. A policy is a course of action, often action to be taken in the present or the near future. So one factor which governs decisions about the purchase of a survey tends to be *timeliness*: the more quickly a survey can be completed the better a client is pleased. The other factors that govern market decisions for most commodities, including surveys, are *cost* and *quality*. Timeliness and cost are readily quantified and easily measured: a survey is offered to a client by a given time at a given price. But quality is not so easily measured. 'In the case of most products of poor quality', writes Rothman 'when they start to perform badly the effect is apparent. The car does not start, the bridge collapses, the computer malfunctions, but research is only one link in a network leading to a decision. Even if it is established that a decision is poor . . . it will still not be clear which of the links in the network performed badly' (1980: 417). And if it is so hard to judge quality after the event it must be at least as hard to judge it beforehand.

Quality of a survey has both a data-construction and a data-interpretation aspect. Good data construction obviously goes to waste if the sample design has failed to identify the right cases to measure or if, with a good design, the response rate is so poor that the measured cases are not representative of the survey population. Equally it goes to waste if the data are faultily analysed or not presented in a way that is comprehensible and relevant to the client. But the converse is also true: no matter how fine a sample design, how high a response rate, how subtle a data analysis, or how interesting a research report, if the survey cases have not been measured validly the data interpretation is worthless. The data-interpretation aspects mentioned here are, relatively, much easier to assess as to quality than the data-construction aspects. The end-products of sampling and statistical analysis, namely, a response rate and a survey report, are highly visible and, in the case of the former, almost as easily interpretable as a measure of time or money. The sample design and the plan for data analysis, while less immediately visible and interpretable, under attack can fall back on the prepared defences of probability theory and its applications to sampling and statistical analysis. To a considerable extent, therefore, the data-interpretation aspect of survey quality can hold its own when a client is weighing up the factors of time, cost and quality in deciding what survey to buy. The data-construction aspect of quality, however, is peculiarly vulnerable. On the whole, timeliness and cheapness are positively correlated: the shorter the deadline by which survey results are required and hence the quicker the survey, the cheaper it is likely to be. But data quality, precisely because it requires attention to be given to the construction of each individual datum, is both time-consuming and expensive to achieve: pre-survey pilot work to develop the best questioning strategies takes time, interviewing is expensive, post-survey coding of answers recorded word for word again takes time.

The timeliness/cheapness factor, therefore, seems to be in direct conflict with the data-quality factor; it appears to be impossible to maximise both simultaneously. Or is it? Survey data can, of course, be constructed quickly and cheaply. No pilot work is needed if the questions and the methods of asking them have already been worked out. No interviews are needed if the survey can be conducted through the post. No post-survey coding is needed if the informants can be persuaded to enter the codes themselves. Furthermore, no researcher with experience in data construction would maintain that quick and cheap data cannot be good. The problem that faces the client in making his market-place decision is deciding which data-construction procedures are required for his particular survey purpose. There is no immediately visible indicator of data quality; as I have argued above, all survey data are hard to validate by traditional means and some are impossibly hard. And, unlike the case of sample design or statistical analysis, there is no theoretical position to which the client can have recourse: data-construction theory remains to be formulated. As a result, the factor of data quality is always in danger of being swamped by the instantly measurable factors of timeliness and cheapness. Market forces press always towards a reduction of data quality.

For lack of a good measure of data quality, a survey is usually assessed for quality by examining its data-interpretation procedures. Here is another source of pressure leading to a fall in the validity of data. This is shown most clearly in the editing of survey data. From the standpoint of sampling or statistical analysis, a good-quality survey is one in which each applicable cell of the data matrix contains a value from the range of legitimate values specified for the variate concerned. In such a survey the data are relevant – that is to say, they are potentially valid in that they have the structural properties required to satisfy the client's needs for knowledge. What makes them actually valid is to possess accuracy as well as relevance – that is to say, for each case to take not *any value* from the range of legitimate values for a variate but the specific value that corresponds to the state of the social world. Editing is the final stage in data construction. It consists of a systematic review of all the cells in the data matrix aimed at detecting and correcting any errors that may have crept into the data so far in their construction. These errors, of course, constitute either departures from relevance or departures from accuracy (or departures from both).

Editing can do very little to detect, and still less to correct, departures from accuracy. For detection it is limited to the few logical or empirical internal-consistency checks between paired items that can be included in any one survey, and for correction it relies upon an assumption, often arbitrary, about which member of an inconsistent pair is to be regarded as right and which as wrong. Inevitably most survey data are not edited for departures from accuracy; their accuracy, therefore, is taken for granted. All survey data, by contrast, may be edited, and usually are, for departures from relevance. To detect a departure from relevance is essentially a mechanical task, but to correct it is quite another matter. Correction, after all, means the assignment of a case to a specific value on a variate. That value is given by the social world and, for a survey datum proper, is only accessible from an informant (by definition). But by the stage of editing the informant has already supplied his information, it has been used to construct a provisional datum, and this datum has been found wanting. The new, allegedly 'correct' datum that is constructed by the editor to fill the cell in the data matrix is based not on information about the case in whose row this cell falls but upon something else. The datum is now relevant and meets the basic requirements of the sample design and statistical analysis. But there are no grounds for claiming it is accurate. A valid datum, it should be remembered, is one that is both relevant and accurate. Entering values that have been corrected in this way, therefore, makes the survey seem of better quality on the data-interpretation indicators while actually reducing the proportion of valid data in the data matrix. (This argument is taken further in Chapter 8.)

If we conclude, then, that survey data hitherto have been valid enough for the clients who commission them, as shown by the high level of demand for surveys, even though client satisfaction may be based largely on the flimsy evidence of election forecasts, we cannot assume that the data will continue to be valid enough in future. Evidence of validity is needed in order to counteract the ever-increasing pressures towards a decline in the quality of survey data.

Data Validation Needed for Other Users

This evidence is particularly necessary if we consider the needs of other users of survey data beyond the originating clients. We have to ask: *valid enough for whom*? Although surveys are produced in the first instance to meet the practical, policy-related needs of the clients, the best surveys are increasingly nowadays being deposited in archives for analysis by secondary users. And though the needs for data validity of future users are of no concern to the originating client, they should be heeded by responsible researchers. The survey research profession emerged from, and is part of, the larger community of social scientists. Social scientists cannot often commission their own social surveys but can make excellent use of data originally constructed for quite other purposes. Just as the applications of natural scientific technique to commercial or military ends have aided the growth of pure natural science, so applied surveys of the social world can aid the development of social science. Researchers attempt to satisfy the needs of the social science community as well as those of the clients who commission surveys. Bailar and Lanphier, in an appendix to their review of the quality of surveys in the USA, point out some of the conflicts that may arise in consequence. They refer to 'a certain tension' between researchers and government clients 'as to how much time and money can be devoted to the gathering of information which admits a certain completeness in the description of a given subject, but which does not serve any immediate policy-oriented purpose' (Bailar and Lanphier, 1978: 80). Later they contrast the client, who will 'tend to feel the work is completed' when he has received 'a series of progress reports indicating the probable trend of the final results ... or even a brief verbal report of the findings', with the researcher, who, 'as a result of his commitments to scientific goals and professional peers', will want to produce a much fuller final report (ibid.: 83). Certainly, the social scientist needs a high degree of validity in the data that he is going to spend weeks or months poring over and wants to be warned off data of low validity.

Behind the secondary users of survey data there looms the presence of perhaps the most legitimate user of all – society, the general public, which has a vested interest in the entire survey effort. Society is the subject-matter of surveys and is the researcher's indispensable source of information. If surveys are done *of* society and *by* society (not to mention *at the expense of* society, in every sense), then surely they should be done *for* society also. This is not the place for a detailed discussion of the role of social surveys in social science, but it is necessary to stress that survey researchers, more than the practitioners of any other social science method, are brought face-to-face with the problem of their relationship to the public because they rely on the public to give them information. Direct observers may spy ('unobtrusively'), experimenters can manipulate, but survey researchers have to maintain an open relationship, as between equals, with the public. Each has a vital contribution to make: the public to provide information, and the researcher to put the pieces together and feed them back to the public. Social science, then, cannot be for the survey researcher a store of special knowledge secreted in the heads of a priestly caste of social scientists, who from time to time dispense bits of it to an ignorant public. Rather it must be society gaining increasing knowledge of itself. This approach to social science has implications for data construction that are further explored in Chapter 6 in connection with the requirement for the informant to be willing to perform the task he is set. In the short run it may have implications for the vexed issue of the general fall in response rates due to refusals, which has been experienced in many countries. Bailar and Lanphier write of a survey in which the informants were told they would be sent the results for their region. This proved 'very successful in increasing response rates over previous years when the incentive was not offered' (Bailar and Lanphier, 1978: 51). If society is to be seen as a sort of tertiary user of survey data, then the data must be valid enough to meet its needs. If we require good information from the public, then we owe the public good data in return.

Validation of Process

It seems, then, that validity of survey data cannot be taken for granted, that when clients commission surveys they need to know about the quality of data they are going to receive and that all subsequent users of a survey also need to know the quality of the data laid before them. If their needs are to be satisfied a means of testing data for validity is required.

Applying the traditional 'validation of results' approach discussed at the beginning of this chapter, the researcher should ideally be able to say about the entry in any cell in his data matrix: 'This is a valid datum; *ergo*, the act of measurement of this case on this variate worked.'

Obviously, in practice, a researcher would not want to test every datum for validity. To do so would imply that he already possessed a valid entry (a measured criterion value or a theoretically predicted value) for every cell, in which case his survey would be superfluous. But what no doubt every researcher who cares for the quality of data would like to be able to say is that he had tested a random sample of data from every column in his data matrix against valid standard values and that such-and-such a percentage (he would hope 100 per cent) in such-and-such a column was found to be valid. If the values on the variate were arranged in an ordinal or quantitative manner, he could also say something about the direction and distance of any departures from validity that he had discovered. The conclusion he would like to present would be: 'These are valid data – *ergo*, the mode of measurement used to measure this variate in this survey worked.' (The terms 'act of measurement' and 'mode of measurement' are explained further on p. 71)

Unfortunately, the 'validation of results' approach does not permit such a test to be made and such a conclusion to be drawn for the reasons already given: direct observation cannot provide criterion values for more than a small fraction of the social world; surveys of the post-enumeration type cannot establish valid criterion values; and construct validation, which can only work where theory is already articulated, cannot provide results at the datum level.

At this point, perhaps, the prospects for validation look bleak. But do they need to do so? Validation of results may be difficult but there is no doubt that researchers, especially those who are close to the data-construction work, are able to tell good data from bad. They do so all the time in connection with the daily routine of their own surveys and other surveys that they come in contact with. They know, as the people involved, how easy it is to produce shoddy data even if it may be very hard actually to document, by comparison with standard values, that the data are shoddy. What they do is to give their attention to the *processes by which the data are constructed*. They make comments like the following: The question is confusing ... It doesn't explain what we want ... I don't understand what it means, so how can an informant be expected to? ... It's too long ... Informants will only listen to the first half of it ... They won't know the answer ... Interviewers will miss it out if it's tucked away at the bottom of the page ... The grid format is too complicated ... The layout is awkward ... It's easy enough to ask in the office but not with an old lady who's deaf ... There's no room to write an answer in ... The 'no' code is put before the 'yes' code ... The codes are printed too close together ... The code symbols are too far from the definitions ... The continuity instruction isn't clear ... Where are you supposed to go next if the informant says 'maybe' instead of 'yes' or 'no'? ...

Such a list of typical comments could be extended almost indefinitely. Those listed apply only to the questions as printed in the questionnaire. Other comments would cover the subject matter of the survey (for example, income, expenditure, employment, education, housing, health – the different topics present different problems); the aspects of the subject-matter that were being asked about (for example, opinions or behaviours); the recruitment, basic training and supervision of the interviewers and coders; the specific briefing and training given to interviewers and coders on the survey in question and what sorts of checks were made of their work; pre-tests of the questions; the sequences of topics in the questionnaire; the design of the coding frames; the edit checks that were made. In this way, a detailed critique of the data is prepared concentrating upon the long series of choice points at which specific decisions have to be taken in the very complex process of constructing a survey datum. These decisions, minute though some of them may seem, can make or mar a survey datum. A wrong decision is very likely to destroy the validity of a datum irretrievably; good decisions at other choice points will not save it.

An interesting feature of the researchers' comments is that no two are likely to be the same; *quot homines, tot sententiae*. Hedges writes that he has 'often polished a draft questionnaire to the stage at which I think it is entirely satisfactory for its purpose. I have then submitted it to colleagues for discussion, only to find that they can quickly spot many flaws . . . ' (1982: 59) Most researchers have had this experience. Furthermore, one's colleagues are likely to differ among themselves as to the points they make. It is not that some of the comments will be right and others wrong so much as that different aspects will be concentrated upon by different people. Their different special interests and experiences (for example, in interviewing, coding, or data preparation for computer processing) will give them different cognitive schemata and they will, as a result, perceive the data-construction processes differently. However, underlying these differences there is a basic similarity of approach won from a common attempt to grapple with the problems of data construction.

When survey data are faulty they are often dramatically faulty, so that the practitioner who is having to deal with them cannot escape becoming aware that there is something wrong. And once the fault is detected it is often again quite dramatically clear what the nature of the problem was that produced the fault. This is especially the case with coders and editors (often the same people) who, in the relatively cloistered calm of a coding department, can see what may not have been so clear to an interviewer in the hurly-burly of an interview in the informant's house or workplace. In a well-conducted coding unit the individual coders are taught never to generate their personal *ad hoc* solutions to coding problems but to refer them to their coding supervisor who will ensure that a consistent approach is applied. The supervisor often finds a batch of almost identical problems being referred, and it is almost instantly obvious where the data-construction procedure has gone awry (though it may not be at all obvious what can be done after the event to remedy the situation).

There is, therefore, already in existence a sort of implicit theory of data construction to which the practitioners have recourse in devising their own procedures and judging those of their colleagues. Data construction is a complex matter but not deeply mysterious. Any full-time practitioner who develops an interest in, and a commitment to, the work becomes privy to this implicit theory – perhaps first beginning to develop it for himself and then discovering that his experiences, and his conclusions from his experiences, are in great measure shared by fellow practitioners in his own and other survey research organisations.

A solution to the problem of validating survey data would be to make this implicit theory explicit and to derive from it principles that could be regarded as standards against which the data-construction procedures actually employed in a survey could be compared. 'Criterion' and 'construct' validation are not appropriate for general use on survey data but there is another approach taken in the assessment of psychological tests which, in its general outlook though not in its detailed application, comes closer to what is required for survey data validation. This is known as 'content validation'. It is used for tests to which criterion and construct validation do not apply – for example, to decide whether an item like 'What is two times two?' is an appropriate part of a test of mathematical achievement. The content of the item is compared with the intended content of the test as a whole. As Nunnally says, it 'rests mainly on appeals to reason' – a very different matter from the kind of appeal to common sense that is made in 'face validation'. He adds: 'In spite of the efforts of some to settle every issue about psychological measurement by a flight into statistics, content validity is mainly settled in other ways' (Nunnally, 1967: 82–3).

These other ways are also applicable in surveys. Content validation is almost literally the approach taken in what I have called the first phase of data interpretation, when the needs for knowledge of the client, expressed at a high conceptual level, are reduced to the variates of the data matrix at a conceptual level appropriate to informants. By analogy with content validation, the method here suggested for validating survey data might be called 'process validation'. It requires a set of principles based not on arbitrary whim nor yet on a mere plain man's common sense, but rather on an understanding of the data-construction process. The aim would be to construct a methodological catechism according to which any survey datum could be interrogated. In looking directly at the procedures of a survey it would reverse the direction of argument in validation of results: instead of 'data valid, *ergo* process valid', it would argue 'process valid, *ergo* data valid'.

The weakness of the approach is apparent. Use of good procedures in making something does not absolutely guarantee the quality of the finished product. But where, as most of the time in surveys, there is no direct test of the quality of the product, surely it is better to have some formal testing of the procedures through which the product was produced than none at all. Better to buy a house sight unseen with a guarantee of the architect's design and the builder's workmanship than without. Either way it may fall down but its chances of survival are better in the former instance than in the latter.

Advocacy of process validation does not mean dismissing the importance of criterion and construct validation where they can successfully be done, especially in the testing of survey measures before they are used rather than after the event, when it is too late to set them right. The process-validational approach has the advantage that it can be applied to all survey data, both in advance of the data construction, when the procedures are being planned, and after the data matrix is filled. According to Marsh (1982), the increase in recent years in automatic accounting and stock control means that the field that is increasingly becoming the focus of attention in market research is subjective phenomena (attitudes, evaluations, and so on). It is in this internal part of the social world that validation of results has least role to play and that process validation is most needed (at least by those who wish to see these data subjected to some kind of test of validity).

Process validation is of particular importance to secondary users of data. The original client and researcher may be well aware of the limitations of their own data but these are not necessarily so apparent to another user. One data matrix may be superficially very like another, even where the quality of the data in the cells varies greatly between the two. It is important to bear in mind that validity is not a property that data carry around with them from one use to another: data that are relevant to one user and that are accurate enough to meet his needs for knowledge may fail on one or the other score when the knowledge needs of another user are to be served. The secondary user must be able to carry out his own validational check of the data.

One feature of a descriptive technique like the social survey, very noticeable to an experimentalist entering the field of survey research, is the absence of built-in internal alarm signals to show when the system fails. An experimenter may lavish a great deal of care on his experiment and ask himself: Has he made a strong induction of his independent variable? Has he devised a sensitive measure of his dependent variable? Has he introduced controls in order to forestall possible alternative explanations of his findings? But, at the end, even if all such questions are answered to his satisfaction, his experiment will be measured by the differences he obtains on his dependent variable: no differences, no dice – the experiment fails. A survey, however, hardly ever fails on account of its findings. Because 'validation of results' is so difficult to carry out, the data of surveys escape the stringent test that all experimental data are subject to. One might think that it is all the more important, therefore, that the procedures of a survey – the means by which the data are generated – should be given a searching scrutiny before the data are accepted. But such a scrutiny does not usually occur; so long as the procedures are even remotely adequate the findings tend to be accepted. Often the only indicators of success that are looked at are the sample size and the response rate. The result is that, to the lay user, all surveys appear to be equal in quality. This shows up in reports of surveys in newspapers and even in the pages of a popularising social science magazine like *New Society*, where side by side one may read a report of a meticulously conducted, highly professional piece of survey research and a report of a study which, to the practised eye, offers many tell-tale signs of careless data-construction procedure. Noelle-Neumann (1980) points to a similar lack of discrimination between good and poor data of opinion research in the news media in West Germany.

The difference, of course, between the experimentalist and the survey researcher in the capacity of their research techniques to fail flows from the more modest aims of the latter. He is out to describe a reality already known to exist; the experimenter is testing the existence of a new reality that he is claiming to exist but now must prove. The survey researcher is like a land surveyor, who is bound to return with some kind of description of the land he surveys; the experimenter is like a mineral prospector, who may very well return empty-handed. The prospector proves his success by displaying a nugget of gold; the land surveyor does not prove the quality of his work by presenting his description but must produce independent evidence as to the procedure he followed.

The good data constructor, therefore, must pay constant attention to methodology. (I use this word to mean the science or theory of method, not just an account of methods, as it is sometimes used.) Saying this contradicts not only much routine practice by survey researchers but also a well-known warning given by Max Weber in 1905:

Methodology . . . is no more the precondition of fruitful intellectual work than the knowledge of anatomy is the precondition for 'correct' walking. Indeed, just as the person who tried to govern his mode of walking continously by anatomical knowledge would be in danger of stumbling so the professional scholar who attempted to determine the aims of his own research extrinsically on the basis of methodological reflections would be in danger of falling into the same difficulties. (Weber, 1949: 115)

What Weber meant by methodology, however, was something much more abstract and detached from research practice than methodology as I am conceiving it. As his discussion of the historian Eduard Meyer's methodology shows, he meant something more like 'philosophy of science'. But philosophy of science, as usually conducted, seems of little help to the practising researcher. It is too far removed from the fray, formulated by strategists who at best draw lessons from the last war but one, and not infrequently teach the art of tilting at windmills.

The need for methodology as a codification of ongoing research practices is argued by Lazarsfeld and Rosenberg in the classic 'General Introduction' to their 1955 reader. Perhaps with Weber in mind, they begin that introduction with the fable of the centipede who lost his ability to walk when asked the order in which he moved his feet. In their version he had been asked by a methodologist, who had better luck with other centipedes and raised the general level of walking in the centipede community. But walking, whether by a centipede or a human, or indeed any other form of locomotion, is not a good analogy of social research. The problem is that social research can give the appearance of taking you from point A to point B when in fact the journey has not been accomplished. Nothing is easier than for a researcher to claim success in his travels ('Look, I was at A and now I'm at B! I started with a problem; now I have a solution'). The crucial question is: Has he reached a real or illusory B? If there is an umpire to register his arrival at a reception point we have criterion validation. Or if his account of the geography of B squares with our general knowledge of the terrain we can say we have construct validation. But more often in social science no one has previously reached this spot and very little is known about its general features. Under these conditions we have to ask questions about his capacity for making the journey. Was he wearing the right clothing, carrying the best equipment? Did he know how to navigate? Validation of results argues back from the correctness of a conclusion to the correctness of the method employed to reach that conclusion. Process validation must argue from the theoretical correctness of a method to the correctness of the results obtained.

The putting into practice of a systematic process validation places two requirements upon the researcher. Since its aim is to enable the researcher (or his client or some other interested user) to check whether the procedures actually used conform to the principles of good data construction, it requires statements of these principles and of the procedures used, so that the two may be compared. A systematic statement of the principles of data construction does not, at present, exist although there is a voluminous literature of tentative steps in that direction. In my view it is self-evident that such a statement of principles must flow out of a theory of data construction (that is, how to do it well must flow out of an understanding of how to do it at all), and the lack of the former is due to the lack of the latter. In Part Two of this book an attempt is made at remedying some of these deficiencies. Statements of data-construction procedures employed in specific surveys are also sparse and often inadequate, perhaps because the researcher has not been entirely clear to whom he was addressing the statement or for what purpose. In the remainder of this chapter I shall first take a quick look at how data-construction theory has developed hitherto and what it is required to do, and then discuss the problem of reporting data-construction techniques in such a way as to facilitate process validation.

The Slow Development of Data-Construction Theory

There can be little doubt that a theory of data construction in social surveys is needed. Cochran wrote: 'The purpose of sampling theory is . . . to develop methods . . . that provide, at the lowest possible cost, estimates that are precise enough for our purpose' (1953: 5). Paraphrasing this, one could say that the purpose of data-construction theory is to develop methods that provide, at the lowest possible cost, data of good-enough quality for our purposes. Yet rather little progress has been made. Kurt Lewin, not a survey researcher himself, wrote in 1943 that 'we need most urgently a real theory of questionnairing and interviewing which offers more than a few technical rules' (Lewin, 1951: 163). And Deming, a year later, very much from inside the survey field and writing in a sociological journal, stressed the 'need for workable theories of bias and variability in response just as much as there ever was need for theories of sampling bias and sampling errors'. He called for a 'thorough-going plan of theoretical and experimental investigation' which, he said, 'would pay dividends in money, not to speak of dividends in scientific self-respect of the statistician' (Deming, 1944: 360).

Forty years on, not much has been achieved. Tropp, in his address to the annual conference of the Social Research Association in London in 1979, pointed to a need, still not satisfied, for 'a theoretical understanding of what is happening at various stages of the survey research situation' (*SRA News*, January 1980: 7). Payne's *The Art of Asking Questions*, first published in 1951, was republished, unrevised, in 1980 – a tribute not just to the readability and general good sense of the book but also to the lack of development in what Lewin called 'questionnairing' in the intervening years. A science that is making satisfactory progress ought not to be able to reproduce unchanged after that length of time a book of practical hints except as a historical curiosity. But in the 1980s Payne's is probably still the best and most practically useful book of its kind. Techniques of data construction are not demonstrably better today than they were in 1951. (It is sobering to note that Woodward, reviewing Payne's book in 1952, expressed the hope that it would 'be as badly out of date in 1962 as 1942 questionnaires are today'.)

Schuman and Presser have drawn attention to the fact that a number of question-wording experiments were carried out in the 1940s but that by the early 1950s they had largely disappeared. As one reason for this decline they mentioned 'the ad hoc character of most of the early work [in which] larger theoretical issues of question construction and typology were seldom addressed' (Schuman and Presser, 1978: 29). It is true that, during the period they refer to, a definitive theory did not emerge but the fact is that probably more was done then to develop theory in the data-construction field than has been done since. The 1930s and 1940s saw a rapid expansion in the use of the social survey method in both Britain and the USA. In the prewar years George Gallup introduced the systematic polling of public opinion, and the survey method was increasingly applied in commercial research. The exigencies of war led to a large programme of social research within the US army, organised by Samuel Stouffer (reported by Stouffer *et al.*, 1949/50), and to the setting up in Britain, under Louis Moss's direction, of an official survey research agency which has survived, with various changes of title, to the present day. This expansion of survey work provided fertile ground for the growth of new ideas about the data-construction procedures.

The person most responsible for the theoretical advance was Paul Lazarsfeld, surely the most innovative and creative worker that social survey method has known. His English-language publications between 1934 and 1951 contained a wealth of theoretical ideas about aspects of the data-construction process. One feature of his work is that it dealt both with questions and with answers – both, that is to say, with problems of questionnaire design and with problems of the classification of survey responses. For instance, his chapters in the 1937 textbook on market research, prepared by a committee of the American Marketing Association on which he sat, included two on questionnaire design (chapters 3 and 4), one on classification (chapter 11) and one on the interpretation of data (chapter 15). (All the headings to these chapters included the word 'psychological'. Psychology, Lazarsfeld realised, is the discipline on which a theory of data construction must be founded.)

These ideas, however, were not linked to form a systematic theoretical approach, and this may well be why the flood of experiments on question wording that also occurred in this period dried up. It takes a theory to sustain practice and no systematic theoretical base had been laid. I suspect that there are two main reasons why this burst of theoretical work came almost to an end in the early 1950s. One is that there seems to have been a radical shift in the research interests of Lazarsfeld himself around 1950. The bibliography prepared by Neurath (1979) places Lazarsfeld's books and articles under various topic headings, two of which cover his writings about social research. One of these, 'Social Research: Methods and Procedures', containing his writings dealing with problems of data construction, usually in a market research context, has thirty-one items published before 1950 and twenty-one published later (including books consisting of articles prepared in the earlier period). The other, 'Social Research: Perspectives and Reflections', contains seventy-three books or articles published in 1950 or later and only five published before. (Another of Neurath's topic headings, 'Mathematical Sociology', consists entirely of publications from the later period.) The virtual cessation of the development of data-construction theory around 1950 seems to have been at least in part a consequence of the switching of efforts of its most prominent theorist to his latent-structure analysis, his administrative duties as head of the Bureau of Applied Social Research at Columbia University, and his role of semi-official sage of social science.

Why, though, did other people not take up the theoretical challenge and attempt to integrate the results of the experimental studies of the 1940s, and to advance the nascent data-construction theory? I suspect that the other reason why data-construction theory failed to develop is to be found in the advent of the high-speed electronic computer. Suddenly, all sorts of statistical analyses that had hitherto not been practicable became feasible, and the methodological effort that before had been spread over a much broader front was now concentrated in the narrower quantitative phases of the work. This has been to the detriment of the qualitative side of survey research, including data construction, not only because it diverted attention from the area that most needed attention but because the tool that should be the servant of the researcher threatens always to become master and to dictate how the rest of the work should be done. I have shown already how in editing data a kind of mechanical application of the *relevance* requirement can steam-roller the requirement of *accuracy* and produce data that are actually of reduced validity. This is the sort of misconstruction of data that the computer temptingly lends itself to and that only a strong theoretical bulwark can resist.

This is not to say that methodological research in the data-construction area ended around 1950. The pages of the *Public Opinion*

Quarterly and of the various market research journals provide abundant testimony to the fact that work continued. The main names, with some representative references, are, on question design and interviewing, Fothergill and Willcock (1953), Hyman *et al.* (1954), Gray (1956), Cannell and Kahn (1968), Belson (1981), Bradburn, Sudman *et al.* (1979), Schuman and Presser (1981), Kalton and Schuman (1982); and on coding, Minton (1969), and Kalton and Stowell (1979). It seems fair to say, however, that to a great extent the creative theoretical energy of the earlier period was lost. Researchers have tended to concentrate their efforts on specific subparts of the data-construction field and the result has been an uneven treatment of the field as a whole. Much work has been done on questions and questioning, less on coding and data-construction aspects of editing, and I am not aware of any that has continued Lazarsfeld's theoretical analysis of the classification of survey answers. To my mind, the two greatest theoretical contributions of the post-Lazarsfeld period have been:

(1) The analysis of the survey interview as social interaction by Maccoby and Maccoby (1954) and by Cannell and Kahn (1953, 1957 with order of authors reversed, and 1968), followed and extended by Cannell and his colleagues' testing and further development of hypotheses arising from their theoretical analysis of the interview (Cannell, Marquis and Laurent, 1977, briefly summarising an extensive programme of research conducted between 1959 and 1970; Cannell, Oksenberg and Converse, eds, 1979, reporting more fully studies performed between 1971 and 1977).
(2) The magisterial opus of Galtung (1967), organised around the notion of the data matrix. (In my terminology his Part 1 deals with data construction and Part 2 with data interpretation, but his subject-matter was all social research and not just the social survey.)

Tasks of Data-Construction Theory
Data construction begins when the data matrix of cases and variates has been designed and ends when this matrix has been filled with values. Data-construction theory worthy of the name must cover all the operations carried out in the filling of a survey data matrix and must encourage analytical investigations of all these operations. It must therefore rectify the present unevenness in treatment of these operations. In addition to covering all the data-construction operations it must cover all qualities of survey data; it must be a theory of the data-construction process, not just of response effects or failures of that process. If we understand how data are constructed, we

should be able to understand how errors arise and how they can be avoided.

Data-construction theory has an important linking function. It must attempt to organise and discipline the vast empirical literature of one-shot, untheoretical studies. Many workers in this field have called for controlled experiments. Moser and Kalton say that, by comparison with sampling, 'our knowledge of data collection . . . is primitive. The choice of a particular method or of a question form is based mainly on experience, opinion, and common sense', and they call for 'direct experimentation' (1971: 481–2). But experiments, to be of value, must be tests of general ideas applicable outside the particular experimental setting. In the terminology of Campbell and Stanley (1963), they must have 'external validity'. This validity comes from the location of the separate studies in a larger theoretical structure and, in the past, such a structure has been lacking. Data-construction theory must provide such an integrating structure.

Another form of linking needed is between the routine practice of actual surveys and the conduct of methodological experiments. At present, many researchers go about their business almost entirely ignorant of the methodological literature, and the experimenters often show an astonishing unawareness of how survey data are actually constructed. This is a reflection of the separation between the commercial world of applied survey research and the university-based world of academic social science departments. Organisations like the long-established Survey Research Center at the University of Michigan and the much younger Survey Methods Centre set up by Social and Community Planning Research and City University, London, constitute important attempts to break down this separation, but the problem has to be tackled at a theoretical, as well as an organisational, level. Process validation requires both practical work on surveys and an awareness of the experimental results, the two joined in a common framework of concepts.

A further link that data-construction theory must provide is between routine practice on one survey and on another. At present, in the absence of a theoretical understanding of the entire data-construction process, the researcher, who is very likely working under great time pressure, tends to work hand-to-mouth in devising his data-construction procedures. Rather than risk the undoubted pitfalls of introducing an entirely new and untested measure he borrows from a previous survey a measure that 'worked' last time. But the fact that it worked last time is no proof that it will work again. One cannot generalise from particular to particular directly but must go via a general concept that embraces both particulars. If the two survey situations can be seen to be conceptually identical then it is perfectly correct to say that a procedure that was successful in one should be successful in the other also. To generalise without the conceptual analysis is to act on blind faith and may lead to disaster: the fact that one red berry was edible does not mean the next one will be. In terms of the model I am introducing in this book, a measure can only be transferred from one survey to another if the client's knowledge needs are (essentially) the same on both surveys, the social world is (essentially) unchanged, and the informants and research personnel meet the conditions for good survey task performance to be outlined in Part Two. Generalisation requires a foundation of theoretical analysis.

If it is the case that a successful procedure cannot be carried automatically from one survey to another it must also be the case that an unsuccessful procedure should not be blindly copied. Yet, because of the difficulty of validation, procedures are often repeated without any evidence that they worked last time. Frequency of use is then taken as an indication of validity, with the consequence that the more often error has occurred in the past, the more likely it is to occur again. Like the courtiers who surrounded Louis XVIII, researchers sometimes seem 'to have forgotten nothing and to have learned nothing'. It is only on the basis of a theoretical analysis of the data-construction procedures of a survey that a decision can be taken as to whether a method should be kept the same or changed. On surveys conducted continuously or repeated at intervals, the aim of which is to produce statistical time series, the tendency is always to repeat the procedure used the first time, the object being to ensure that a change in the survey results is due to a change in the trait measured and not to a change in the method of measurement. But if the conditions under which the survey is conducted have changed, then to cling rigidly to a standard procedure may produce the very 'methods artefact' that the researcher wishes to avoid: if someone is observing an object and an obstruction is placed between himself and the object the best way to continue the observation may be for the observer to change his position. The kind of adaptation of methods of measurement over time that I am saying may be necessary for the construction of good data can only be carried out successfully if the researcher has a thorough theoretical understanding of the data-construction process.

I have described the breadth of coverage that data-construction theory must have and its role in linking experiments and routine practices. A further task for it is to organise and evaluate the commonsense rules of thumb that have been much cited in textbooks and, to a lesser extent, applied in practice to guide data-construction work. Which are true and which are not? Which are important and which are not? The standing of four of these rules of thumb will now be explored at some length.

Hitlin reports a test of three 'generally accepted working rules' which he calls (rightly) part of the 'conventional wisdom' about question wording (1976: 39). His test was incorporated into an opinion survey conducted in Washington, DC, in July 1974. The rules that he tested were (1) that a question asking for an evaluation of a person should not be preceded by information about some discreditable action of that person (the evaluation question asked for ratings of Richard Nixon's performance as President, and in the experimental treatment it was preceded by a question asking whether the informant thought Nixon should be impeached and removed from office); (2) that a question asking for an evaluation of a person should not include a reminder of this person's high status (the question asked which of two candidates in an election for mayor the informant intended to vote for, and in the experimental treatment the information was added that one of the candidates was the incumbent mayor); (3) that a question asking about a person's stand on a controversial issue should not include an argument supporting one side of the issue only (the question asked whether the informant supported or opposed the introduction of a state lottery, and in the experimental treatment an argument was included in favour of the lottery). In all three tests the experimental treatment which broke the 'rule' was compared with a control treatment which omitted the rule-breaking elements described above. Informants were randomly allocated to one of the two treat-ments in what researchers on question wording call a 'split-ballot' design. The numbers were reasonably large – about 500 in each treatment for the tests of rules 1 and 3 and about 240 per treatment for the test of rule 2. Although Hitlin's results showed a slight trend in the direction predicted by the rules of thumb on each of the three tests, the differences did not approach statistical significance.

Hitlin's study is useful in showing up the fragility of these rules of thumb. A rule of thumb ought to be a truism – a statement which, though it may be trivial, is always true. If it works on some occasions but not on others it is useless as a rule of thumb. (To be told 'to get from A to B bear east' may be a useful rule, but to be told 'sometimes bear east and sometimes bear west' is certain to be useless.) What one then needs is a statement of the conditions under which it does and does not apply. But such a statement is at a higher conceptual level than the rule of thumb. We are now beginning to talk about a theory, which requires a reasoned application to a practical situation, rather than a simple rule that can be applied almost blindly. At this theo-retical level, Hitlin's three rules all turn out to be instances of the same more general principle – the principle that the researcher, when asking for an opinion held at the present moment, must beware of altering the informant's cognitive schema. If, whether through asking an earlier question or through introducing ideas into the question itself, he feeds information to the informant that the latter previously lacked and this information is relevant to the subject-matter of the question and likely to influence the informant's answer to the question, then the answer given by the survey informant cannot be regarded as representative of opinions held by the larger population to which the client intends the survey results to be generalised.

Hitlin's results throw the rules of thumb into confusion but do not threaten the general principle that the researcher, in a sample survey, must not change the part of the social world that he is measuring. His results illustrate the importance of not working at the rule-of-thumb level but of moving to a more abstract level such as that of the schema. Then one can see that if the social world (the schema in this case) is altered the answers will be affected, but if it is not altered (much, as in Hitlin's tests of the three rules) the answers will not be (much) affected.

Another of the question-wording rules of thumb has been subjected to a probing experimental analysis by Laurent, working in Cannell's research team at the Survey Research Center, University of Michigan. This is the 'rule' that a good survey question should be short. The status of the rule has in fact always been in doubt because it is in logical contradiction with another, equally hallowed, rule – that a good survey question is clear, unambiguous. In my terms, a clear question is one that identifies the case and the variate of the data matrix and that instructs the informant in how he is to match the case to the variate. To achieve this may require the use of many words: clarity is often incompatible with brevity. The two rules have been printed side by side in question-wording manuals, and their incompatibility has not greatly bothered the authors. It is only when one attempts to integrate all the rules of thumb within a common theoretical structure that the incompatibility cannot be ignored and, on further analysis, perhaps begins to become soluble.

The rule that questions should be short often takes the very concrete form of saying that they should not be more than about twenty words in length. This rule has the convenient feature of every good rule of thumb that it can be applied mechanically – it does not require the exercise of research intelligence. It seems to go back to a conclusion that Payne (1951) arrived at from his careful examination of the results of a split-ballot experiment in which the order of alternatives presented was the experimental variable. One half of the sample, for example, were asked 'Do you think that this tax is too high or about right?', and the other half, 'Do you think that this tax is about right or too high?' The experiment contained sixteen questions produced in two versions in this way. Nine of them showed essentially no difference in the distribution of answers due to the difference in the ordering of the alternatives, but seven of them did show statistically significant differences. These seven questions clearly did not work. Both versions of each question were intended to measure the same social world aspect but they obtained different values. Hence the question was unreliable – an incidental attribute, the ordering of the alternatives, was determining the results of the measurement process. One feature that Payne noticed these seven questions shared in common was that they were rather long, varying from 21 to 46 words around an average value of 31, while the other nine, which had not produced order differences, were shorter, ranging from 11 to 26 words with an average of 22. Hence Payne's conclusion that 'we might try to keep our questions somewhere in the neighbourhood of 20 words or less' (1951: 136).

While this recommended maximum word limit was being repeated in methods textbooks in the 1950s and 1960s, often without attribution to Payne, psychologists studying non-research interviews were beginning to discover an interesting dependence of an interviewee's behaviour upon the behaviour of the interviewer. Matarazzo and Wiens (1972) report the findings of a series of experiments carried out in the course of interviews with applicants for the job of patrolman in a large-city police force. They systematically varied the latency of the interviewer's utterances (that is, how long the interviewer waited before beginning to speak after the interviewee had spoken) and found that the interviewee adjusted his own latency to that of the interviewer. They found a similar dependence of the length of the interviewee's response upon the length of the interviewer's question. For instance, in one of eight similar experiments, they carried out 45-minute interviews with each of twenty job applicants using 'non-directive open-ended questions' (Matarazzo and Wiens, 1972: 82) about the applicant's occupation, education and family. The interview was divided into three 15-minute blocks in each of which all three topics were covered. In the first and last blocks the interviewers' questions were preset to be about 5 seconds in duration while in the middle block the questions were about 10 seconds long. They found the average durations of answers given in the three blocks were 24·3, 46·9 and 26·6 seconds. Their finding has been repeated in other laboratory experiments (for example, Koomen and Dijkstra, 1975) and, outside the laboratory, in observational studies of the relationship between the lengths of questions and answers in US presidential news conferences (Ray and Webb, 1966) and in communications between astronauts and groundstaff during space flights (Matarazzo *et al.*, 1964).

Do these results for non-research interviews have any implications for research interviews? There are important differences between, say, job interviews and survey interviews – for example, in job interviews the interviewee does not play an informant role to the same extent as in survey interviews, and there are reward and punishment consequences of the interview for the job applicant that do not exist for the survey informant – but there are also important similarities in the structure, length and content of the two types of interview. It seemed to Cannell that the Matarazzo effect deserved to be investigated in a survey context.

Already Cannell, Marquis and Laurent had found strong relationships between 'the behavior activity level of the interviewer and that of the respondent' and between 'behavioral activity of the respondent and the number of items reported' (1977: 61). If the respondent was modelling his behaviour upon that of the interviewer then the longer the question, the longer perhaps would be the answer. And while a longer answer might be merely repetitive or irrelevant or simply wrong, there was also the possibility that it would provide fuller information than a short answer and therefore would lay the basis for a more accurate datum. Laurent (1972) reported a series of experiments investigating the effects of systematically varying the lengths of survey questions. (Cannell, Marquis and Laurent [1977] describe this work at an earlier stage in its progress.) In all these experiments Laurent's independent variable was question length and he endeavoured to hold the information-provision task set to his informants at a constant level across his experimental conditions. (According to Koomen and Dijkstra [1975], Matarazzo had found that in his relatively unstructured employment interviews the 10-second questions had imposed rather greater information demands upon his interviewees than the 5-second questions.) Laurent's short version of a question consisted of a single sentence (for example, 'What are the things you do to protect your health?'). His long version ended with the same question as the short version but prefaced it with an introductory statement of the same question, or some irrelevant 'filler' statement, or both (for example, 'Our next question asks those things people do to protect their health. This is an additional subject we are getting a few data on. What are the things you do to protect your health?'). His experiments were inserted into health interviews of the standard Cannell type. The questions asked about *health conditions* (injuries, accidents, acute and chronic illnesses and disabilities) and about *health behaviour* (medicines taken, visits to the doctor, and so on), mostly relating to the informant. They included a variety of 'open' and 'closed' types of question.

In one experiment Laurent found no difference in the length, measured in seconds, of responses to short and long versions of the same question, nor indeed in the length of responses to a questionnaire consisting entirely of short questions compared with questionnaires containing mixtures of short and long questions. The Matarazzo effect, therefore, was not obtained and subsequent tests have failed to find it in survey interviews in which the information demands of the parallel short and long versions of the question are strictly controlled. However, Laurent found a difference between the short-questions questionnaire and the mixed-length-questions questionnaire in the percentage of questions which elicited at least one health condition or health behaviour: 29 per cent for the short questions and 40 per cent for the mixed. In another experiment he checked the accuracy of the health information provided against doctors' records and found that the questionnaires containing mixtures of short and long questions were obtaining more accurate answers than the questionnaires with short questions only.

Although further research – by Laurent himself, reported in the same article, by Henson, Cannell and Lawson (1977) and by Bradburn, Sudman *et al.* (1979: ch. 2) – has not yet fully established the dynamics of the question-length effect, there seems no doubt that, under some circumstances at least, long questions produce better data than short ones: the old rule of thumb about the virtue of short questions has been found wanting.

My purpose in presenting this rather detailed account of some of the experimental attacks on data-construction rules of thumb is to challenge the mode of development of data-construction procedures that we have been content with so far. Hitherto, the direction of events has been: practical experience, often in anecdotal form, leading to rules of thumb. What we need is: practical experience systematically gathered, informing a theory from which principles of good data construction can be derived – these then to be tested in specially contrived experiments and by further experience systematically gathered, with a view to improving the theory and the principles and the practice that is guided by these principles.

The systematic gathering of experience seems to have been what Lazarsfeld meant by 'codification' – a term that he and his associates used frequently. For instance, in his introduction to the first edition of Zeisel's *Say It with Figures* he described the book as 'a first step in the direction of codification' of 'procedures which are treated rather casually elsewhere' (Zeisel, 1947: xiii). A key feature of codification is that it makes explicit what formerly had been 'implicit, but not explicitly formulated' (Kendall and Lazarsfeld, 1950: 187). It aims to 'bring out what is consistent about [ongoing research practices] and deserves to be taken into account the next time' (Lazarsfeld and Rosenberg, eds, 1955: 4).

Experience made systematic and explicit, however, still needs to be generalised before we have a theory of data construction. Such a theory must be pitched at a conceptual level below the clouds of 'philosophy of science' and must not aim at a single sweeping formula. On the other hand, if it is to be applicable to all data-construction operations and all qualities of data, if it is to fulfil the linking functions I have described (between empirical studies, between specific survey

procedures and between the empirical studies and the survey procedures) and if it is to be above the level of anecdote and rule of
thumb, it must be quite general – more general certainly than Laz-
arsfeldian codification. At this level of generality it will not be capable
of application by a machine or by an unskilled clerk. Process validation, therefore, will not be capable of being delegated to an administrative functionary; the research imagination of a survey professional will
be needed to set the technical procedures of a survey against principles
established by data-construction theory and to judge whether the
former match the requirements of the latter.

Reporting Data-Construction Procedures: The Need for Transparency of Data

A process validation of the data of a survey requires not only the
statement of a set of principles of good data construction but also the
statement of the procedures employed in that survey to construct the
data. The aim is that the data should be *transparent*: the method by
which they have been constructed should show through. Many users,
of course, have no interest in the method through which their data
were constructed and lack the professional skill needed to interpret
and evaluate it. But they still need some assurance as to the validity of
these data for themselves, so someone who is familiar with their
knowledge needs must carry out a process validation on their behalf
and to do so must be made aware of the method of data construction.

What such a person needs to know will be discussed in more detail in
Chapter 4, where the outlines of a theory of data construction are
sketched. Suffice it to say for now that the documentation of the
data-construction procedures of the survey must be full enough to
enable the process validator to decide, for each individual datum,
whether it meets the user's requirements for relevance and for
accuracy. This does not mean that the validator must be provided with
a natural history of each datum but it does mean that, at the very least,
he should have access to a report on the data-construction procedures
specific to this survey (that is, the questionnaire and any instructions,
written or oral, given to the informants, interviewers, coders and
editors pertaining to this survey – including, importantly, any late
amendments added to these instructions) and a report on the standard
working methods of the survey organisation, covering the methods
employed to recruit, train and supervise the interviewers, coders and
editors. With all this information the validator will find he has a very
good idea of the data-construction operations performed by the survey
organisation but will still know very little about the raw material upon
which the survey organisation works – the informants and their prior
knowledge of the social world. A well-conducted survey, however,
begins with pre-tests in which the survey organisation itself explores

and experiments with this raw material; and the process validator may well require access to reports on any such pre-tests. Again at the very least he may demand an assurance that pre-tests were undertaken and that their findings were used to guide the survey operations.

The validator may have some difficulty in getting access to all this information. He may find that no record of the data-construction procedures exists or that, if it does exist, the survey organisation is reluctant to release it. Commercial pressure may militate against disclosure of survey information. Tauber reports that when he asked his 'former employer, a major package-goods company, if it would be all right for [him] to publish, they said, "If it's something worthwhile, No – don't tell our competitors about it. If it's something that is not worthwhile, No – we don't want our name affiliated with it!"' (1981: 11–12). Tauber was writing about the problem of releasing the *results* of commercial research but the same consideration can apply to the problem of making research *procedures* public – most especially if they are likely to lead the validator to decide that the data under review are invalid.

Tanenbaum and Taylor (undated), writing from the main British survey archive, proposed that survey items should be tagged with their 'conceptual properties'. This would be difficult because of the wide range of possible 'conceptual properties' that a survey item (or variable) might be regarded as possessing, but it would be potentially useful for the secondary user seeking to check the relevance to himself of somebody else's data. What would also be useful, and perhaps would not present as great difficulties, would be to tag each item as to its accuracy. Whereas relevance varies from user to user, accuracy is relatively fixed: a datum either is or is not what it claims to be. In the absence of such an assessment, the user tends to assume that all data within an archive (where surveys are usually deposited entire) are equally accurate. But a practising researcher would often be prepared to admit that some of his variates were measured much more accurately than others. If the items were tagged as 'accurate', 'possibly accurate', or 'inaccurate', the user could then decide for himself (that is, according to his own knowledge needs) whether or not to make use of the less well-constructed data.

As I reach the end of the first part of this book, a philosophical reflection is perhaps in order. My aim is to help increase the value of social surveys to social scientists by showing how surveys may themselves become more scientific. Data construction is, as I have mentioned earlier, the area of survey work often referred to as being 'more art than science'. What makes scientific knowledge distinct from other forms of knowledge is its claim to be cumulative – it does not guarantee an unbroken chain of progress but does guarantee that what changes occur in the corpus of knowledge should constitute, on balance, improvements and not deteriorations in knowledge. It can only be cumulative if two conditions are satisfied. First, there must be a means of separating good accounts of the world studied from bad; this chapter has discussed ways of distinguishing between good and bad survey data. Secondly, there must be a communication from one scientist to another of the knowledge obtained. Science is a highly social form of knowledge. It is the scientific community which decides what the corpus of scientific knowledge is – what new bits will be added and old bits deleted (that is, what are to be regarded as good and bad accounts of the world). But if the scientific community (and from them ultimately the larger community of the general public) is to share this knowledge, it is not only the new results obtained that each individual scientist or scientific working group must communicate to others but the means by which these results were obtained. In addition to results and conclusions about these results, scientific reports contain descriptions of the procedures through which the results were reached. The aim is that other scientists should be able to know both what the original worker found and how he found it, in enough detail that if need be they can repeat the finding. It is only on this basis that science becomes truly social and a generation of scientists can be said to stand on the shoulders of those who came before. Social surveys can only claim a scientific status if their data are made transparent.

Part Two

Towards a Theory of Data
Construction

4

Process Validation

In the first part of this book I have argued that the question of the quality of survey data is a legitimate matter of concern, that data need to be tested for quality and that methods used hitherto for testing them have been less than satisfactory. I have proposed a new approach termed 'process validation', which requires comparison of procedures actually employed with a set of theoretically derived principles, and I have advanced some basic concepts as a contribution to a theory of survey data: that data are 'constructed' rather than 'collected'; that the different data-construction operations must be linked together and seen as a whole; that a survey datum needs to be seen as a report on a social world made to a researcher acting on behalf of a sponsoring client by a member of the public who has neither the expert knowledge of the social world possessed by the client nor the expert skill as an observer of the social world possessed by the researcher; that for a datum to be valid it must be both relevant to the knowledge needs of the client and accurate as an account of the social world; and that the data-construction phase of a survey can usefully be seen as distinct and relatively detached from its data-interpretation phases.

This chapter will review briefly the argument to be developed in Chapters 5, 6 and 7, will introduce some new terminology and will present in greater detail the method of process validation of survey data discussed in Chapter 3. A short 'afterword' (Chapter 8) will draw out the implications for an approach to measurement error of the argument developed in Parts One and Two.

In Part Two it will be useful for some purposes to divide the role of the researcher into two – the researcher-as-classifier, who classifies knowledge acquired in the survey into datum form, and the research director, who sets tasks for the informant and for the researcher-as-classifier and records their outcomes. Just as the terms 'client' and 'researcher' in Part One defined functions that have to be performed if a survey is to take place at all but that are not necessarily found performed by distinct individuals in any actual survey, so here the terms 'researcher-as-classifier' and 'research director' define functions rather than identifiable individuals. An interviewer both extracts information from informants and converts it into data. As extractor of information she acts as a research director; as converter of information into data she acts as researcher-as-classifier. An office coder, while he is coding, is a researcher-as-classifier but while he helps in, say, the design of a coding frame he is a research director.

The client's requirements for a survey are reduced to the form of a case × variate matrix that is to be filled with data. Chapter 5 presents four conditions that must be satisfied in the design of the data matrix if it is to be capable of containing valid data. In that chapter most attention is given to the presuppositions about the social world that are made every time a survey datum is constructed – presuppositions which must be confirmed if the datum is to have a chance of being valid.

The starting point for Chapters 6 and 7 is the recognition that the values on a variate in the data matrix form a scheme for classifying the survey cases. A datum is a classified item of knowledge. The work of classification can be done by one of three people – the informant, the interviewer, or the office coder. The data-construction process can be seen as a series of tasks set by the research director and performed by one of these three people. Every time a datum is constructed one of two types of task is set for the informant – either to produce a datum (Type A) or to produce evidence from which the interviewer or office coder will produce a datum (Type B). The construction of a valid datum presupposes that certain conditions on the work of the inform-ant will be satisfied. If this presupposition is confirmed for a Type A task then the informant should produce the datum. If it is not, then the informant should carry out a Type B task and the interviewer or office coder should produce the datum. When the informant's task is of Type B the research director sets the researcher-as-classifier a datum-production task which presupposes, again, that conditions on the work of the researcher-as-classifier will be satisfied. In an interview survey, the decision as to whether it is the interviewer or the office coder who produces the datum depends on what systems the research director has to put into effect to ensure that these conditions are satisfied. Chapter 7 ends with an examination of the construction of data about behaviour and opinions. Some of the likenesses and differences are brought out and some special problems are looked at.

The argument, then, is that several conditions need to be satisfied, both in designing the data matrix and in carrying out the data-construction process, if valid data are to be the eventual outcome. In particular, if we now put the survey data model in this modified form,

$$\text{CLIENT} - \begin{bmatrix} \text{RESEARCH DIRECTOR} \\ \text{RESEARCHER-AS-CLASSIFIER} \end{bmatrix} - \text{INFORMANT} - \text{SOCIAL WORLD},$$

we can see that the research director, in seeking to provide the client with a knowledge product, is making presuppositions about the social world, the informant and (often) the researcher-as-classifier, all of which must be confirmed if the data are to be valid on which that knowledge product is to be based.

A process validation requires that the data-construction method employed in a given survey should be examined to see whether it satisfies the conditions just referred to. What aspect of the method should be tested? It is useful here to introduce two more terms into the discussion. The data matrix consists of rows (one for each case) and columns (one for each variate) that intersect at individual cells. We shall call the entire set of procedures used to treat with – if possible, to enter a datum in – a single cell of the matrix an 'act of measurement'. The process-validational approach would argue that if the act of measurement for a given cell was good – that is, if it satisfied the conditions on the design of the matrix and on the data-construction process – then there should be a valid datum in that cell. But it is obviously absurd to expect to be able to check every cell in the matrix in this way. More practicably we can apply this approach to each column in the matrix. We shall call the entire set of procedures used to treat with a matrix column – that is, the sum of the separate acts of measurement through which cases are assigned values on the variate for that column – the 'mode of measurement' for the column. It is this which must be reported sufficiently fully to enable a process validation to be made. The data in the column are 'transparent' to the extent that the procedures in the mode of measurement are opened up to a process-validational inspection.

The possible outcomes for any cell in a data matrix column are as follows:

(1) An advance decision that no measurement will be taken, probably because the case does not form a member of the category defined by the variate for this column (see Chapter 5). These are cases to which the variate 'does not apply'.

(2) A non-datum. Here the researcher intended to take a measurement but failed to do so successfully. The outcome is something other than one (only) of the values on the variate. The occurrence of these outcomes gives the process validator cause to wonder about the actual success of the acts of measurement through which data were constructed. (It may also throw the sampling design of a sample survey awry and thus cause a problem at the stage of the interpretation of the data.)

(3) A datum (that is, the case is assigned one of the values on the variate).

A process validation considers the non-data and the data that result from the application of a single mode of measurement. The non-data, being irrelevant by definition and therefore invalid, cast some doubt on the capacity of the mode of measurement to produce good data. The data are relevant by definition but not necessarily accurate. Potentially they may include invalid as well as valid instances. The way to decide about the quality of the data in a column of the matrix is to ask the following questions:

(1) *The design of the data matrix (see Chapter 5)*
    (a) Are its cases, variates and values relevant to the client's knowledge needs?
    (b) Are the variates and values pitched at the appropriate (low) conceptual level?
    (c) Is standardisation achieved down the columns, across the rows and within the cells?
    (d) Are the presuppositions about the social world implied by the matrix confirmed?

(2) *The informant's data-construction task (see Chapter 6)*
    (a) Does the task as formulated (for example, the printed question in the questionnaire) reflect what the data matrix requires? (For Type A: Does it specify the values? For Type B: Does it specify the variate?)
    (b) In an interview survey, do the interventions by the interviewer (probes, feedback, and so on) reflect the task as formulated?
    (c) Are the conditions on good work by the informant satisfied –
        (i) that he should understand his task?
        (ii) that he should be able to perform it?
        (iii) that he should be willing to perform it?
    (d) Is the outcome of the informant's task correctly recorded (for Type A a value; for Type B evidence)?

(3) *The researcher-as-classifier's task (see Chapter 7)*
    (a) Does the coding frame specify the values in the data matrix?
    (b) Are the conditions on good work by the researcher-as-classifier satisfied –
        (i) that he should understand his task?
        (ii) that he should be able to perform it?
        (iii) that he should be willing to perform it?
    (c) Is the value correctly recorded?

If the informant's task is of Type A and the questions under headings (1) and (2) are all answered 'Yes', the mode of measurement passes the test of process validation. If any are answered 'No', it fails. For a Type B task the questions under headings (1), (2) and (3) must all be answered 'Yes' if the mode of measurement is to pass the test.

5

Design of the Data Matrix

If a survey is to be successful the design of the data matrix must satisfy four conditions. These must be satisfied, that is to say, before the question of filling the matrix even arises. This chapter begins with a brief summary of these four conditions. The first is not taken any further but the next three are then elaborated, in order and in some detail. The chapter ends with a discussion of how the conditions for a well-designed data matrix may be secured.

Conditions on the Design of a Data Matrix

(1) The content of the cases in the rows of the matrix and the variates and values in the columns of the matrix must be relevant to the client's original knowledge needs; the aspects of the social world under study in this survey must be those that he wants to have studied. This is the fundamental precondition for a successful survey and does not require any justification or elaboration.

(2) The variates and values of the matrix must be pitched at the (low) conceptual level that is appropriate for data construction.

(3) The same case must be measured throughout any one row of the matrix, and the same variate and values applied throughout any one column. This is the requirement of standardisation.

(4) Each pairing of a case with a variate and its values (that is, each cell in the matrix) implies definite presuppositions about the nature of the social world, which must be confirmed if a valid datum for that cell is to be constructed.

Once these four conditions for the design of the data matrix have been satisfied, the researcher has a potentially valid survey. He now can embark on the design of a mode of measurement for each variate – a set of procedures for filling each column in the matrix. Each mode of measurement must satisfy further conditions about the informants and about the researcher-as-classifier. If all these conditions are satisfied, the survey data are defined as valid.

The Conceptual Level of Survey Data
The client, as an expert on the social world, has specialist knowledge

of the content of the social world, and it is an addition to his knowledge at this high conceptual level that he wishes the survey to provide. No doubt when he looks at the social world directly his expert knowledge of it enables him to perceive it at this high conceptual level. Just as in ordinary life we perceive friendliness in a pattern of facial movements (and do not first perceive the facial movements and then the friendliness), so the survey client, confronted with his own familiar special subject-matter, directly perceives meanings and relationships that would escape the non-expert. As an educational expert he would perceive, say, an 'academic orientation' in a person's pattern of examination results; or as an expert on the social stratification of Britain he would perceive a 'Registrar-General's Social Class III, Manual' in an employed person's combination of occupation as postman and employment status as foreman.

But a social survey is conducted precisely because the client cannot make his own direct perception of the social world. It is too large or too inaccessible for him to observe directly. He therefore has to employ the services of a researcher, who would ideally use his own staff of expert observers to make direct observations of the social world and then report them to the client. But much of this social world is inaccessible to direct observers; the researcher in turn has to call on the assistance of informants, and the whole laborious business of the construction and interpretation of survey data has to take place

Informants, as I have tried to establish earlier, are non-specialist knowers of parts of the same social world on which the client is an expert; they can provide information about it but at a low conceptual level. They can report on a person's examination results, or that he is a postman and a foreman, but they cannot be expected to report on his academic orientation or his Registrar-General's Social Class. Of course, some informants may have these special perceptual skills, but the client needs to have all cases measured, not just some.

The existence of the gap between the conceptual level at which the client works and the conceptual level at which the informant works is one of the fundamental problems of knowledge production in social surveys. The size of the gap may vary from survey to survey as the degree of generality or abstraction of the client's concepts varies but it is always there. The researcher cannot bridge this conceptual gap by elevating the informant's conceptual level to that of the client nor even by making them meet halfway. One of the commonest errors encountered in survey research, indeed in the design of all types of forms that have to be filled in by members of the public, is for a question to an informant to be pitched at a higher conceptual level than that at which his everyday knowledge of the social world is organised. (A principle of data construction to be elaborated later is that the task set to the survey informant must be within his ability to perform.) The problem is not unique to surveys or form-filling but seems often to arise when specialists try to communicate with the public. Baddeley (1981) investigated the effects of an expensive campaign mounted by the BBC to teach radio listeners about changes in wavelengths. Despite frequent repetitions people did not learn the new wavelengths. It seems that all that is needed for everyday use is to be able to find one or two favourite stations, which can be done as effectively by using a scratch or bump on the set to mark the place as by paying attention to the numbers on the dial. Weather forecasters fall into the same trap, insisting on talking about 'troughs of low pressure' when all people want to know for everyday purposes is whether today's temperature is going to be the same as yesterday's, or warmer or colder and whether it is likely to rain. The task for the survey researcher is to come down from the conceptual level required by the client to that at which the informant can operate comfortably.

Nor can this conceptual gap be bridged by the researcher-as-classifier. The researcher is an expert in the measurement of the social world at large but he does not have expert knowledge of any particular aspect of the content of the social world. All measurement ultimately comes down to classification – the assignment of a case to a category that is capable of having more than one member – and much social measurement, as undertaken in surveys, consists of nothing but classification. Measuring a person's age, which constitutes what statisticians call a 'ratio scale' or a 'quantitative' variate, requires classification just as much as does measurement of his marital status – single, married, widowed, or divorced – on a 'nominal scale' or a 'categorical' variate. No matter what assumption is made about the nature of the underlying dimension, a measure when actually applied treats the dimension not as continuous but as consisting of discrete points or regions, at each of which cases may be gathered to form a category or class. (The problems that arise when we try to force this polytomous model on to what is often a continuous universe are touched on later in this chapter.)

Survey data constructors are experts at the classification of the social world. Classification is the art of understanding the rules, which may vary in complexity, for assigning cases to categories and then of applying the rules – the art of picking up the information afforded by these cases that is relevant to the classification task of the moment, discarding all other irrelevant information and assigning the cases to the categories according to the rules. It is a skilled activity, learned over time, and the expert data constructor in a survey organisation acquires the ability to apply it to any aspect of the social world designated in a given survey. Data construction is the transformation of knowledge from its state as information in the head of the informant to its state as classified datum in the data matrix, and it is carried out by the informant, who lacks expert ability as an observer of the social world, under the guidance of and assisted by the researcher.

The characteristic feature of this transformation of knowledge is that it consists of a process of discarding unwanted knowledge. There is an element of knowledge, defined ultimately by the client's knowledge needs and immediately by the definition of the categories on the variate being measured, that is possessed by the informant and that the researcher wants to obtain because it is sufficient to assign a case to a category. All other elements of knowledge held by the informant are, for the moment, irrelevant and to be ignored. The classification process is like the sculptor's carving of a block of stone rather than the potter's shaping of clay: bits are to be removed, not added. The data constructor, like a music-hall comedian, is all the time saying, 'I don't want to know that'.

To bridge the conceptual gap from informant to client, however, requires not a discarding but an adding on of new knowledge. This new knowledge can only be contributed by the member of the survey knowledge-production enterprise who possesses expert knowledge of the aspect of the social world under study. To elevate knowledge from the conceptual level of the informant to that of the client requires a theoretical mastery of this content area, a superplus of knowledge over and above that of the informant. It is a data-interpretation function that must be carried out by client and researcher, working together, after the data have been constructed by the joint team of informant and researcher.

It is useful to think of an 'empirical-theoretical continuum' (Kaplan, 1964: 57; Bulmer, 1979: 657) along which are arrayed concepts at different levels, from the most simple and straightforward (the conceptual level of the variates and values in the survey data matrix) to the most complex and subtle. Data construction is the art of forming the simplest level of concepts from the information provided by survey informants. Data interpretation is the art of working up the continuum from simple to complex concepts. Data interpretation can only be done successfully under theoretical control. In other words, the person who hopes to make useful high-level conceptual interpretations of data must do so from a position of having a theoretical grasp of the social world with which he is dealing. Given this level of understanding he can quite deliberately add assumptions to data.

One of the most widely used of all survey measures in the UK is the Registrar-General's Social Class classification (OPCS, 1980). This measure certainly falls high on the empirical-theoretical continuum. A simple formula is used to code to it: an automatic crossing of two data-level variates (labelled 'occupation' and 'employment status'). Although the operation of crossing the two variates requires no inference process, the next step, the interpretation in terms of Social

Class of each pair of crossed variates, requires a conceptual leap, which is achieved by assuming that a person who falls in a particular cell in the occupation/employment status table is for that reason a member of a particular Social Class and has a position in society appropriate to that Social Class. In effect, the formula for Social Class is not 'SC = Occupation + Employment Status' but rather 'SC = Occupation + Employment Status + Assumptions about Social Position'. Similarly, a person's attitude as measured on a Thurstone scale is not simply a function of his responses of 'agree' or 'disagree' to each statement in a set of opinion statements but of these responses plus a set of assumptions about the way in which interval-level attitude measurement can be arrived at from dichotomous opinion responses. In data interpretation, therefore, the movement up the empirical-theoretical continuum is achieved by adding assumptions to data. By taking thought the knower adds a cubit to the stature of his knowledge.

Data construction, by contrast, has to take care to avoid the making of assumptions – the raising of the conceptual level of information in an untheoretical, uncontrolled way. There is always the temptation to push on to the data-construction phase a process that belongs properly to data interpretation – to expect, for example, informants or interviewers to assign a 'Social Class' or an 'attitude' to a person (in effect, to leap directly from information to expertise) rather than to go through the separate stages of conversion of information to data and then of data to expertise (specialist knowledge). This is not to say that inferential coding, direct movement from the level of information to the level of expertise, cannot take place but that it cannot occur as part of the standard mode of construction of survey data (that is, data based on the contributions of ordinary informants and constructed by a researcher whose own expertise is limited to social observation and who has no special knowledge of the social world). A physician can move directly from a patient's information to a conceptual diagnosis of the patient's medical condition (although he is very likely to supplement this information with some direct observation) but in a survey this sort of inferential coding would have to be done by the client rather than by the informant or the researcher-as-classifier. Data construction, then, is the phase in survey knowledge production that sees a transformation of information into data. In normal circumstances the researcher-as-classifier has only a smattering of specialist knowledge of the social world area surveyed and only to this very small degree is capable of raising the conceptual level of the item of knowledge as it moves from information to datum. Its conceptual level is set by the everyday thought processes of the survey informants and the researcher-as-classifier. It is (ideally) the highest conceptual level at which the least conceptually able of the informants can operate. The raising of the conceptual level of knowledge to the level required by

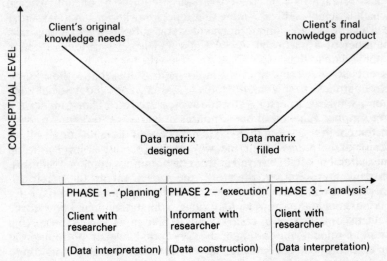

Figure 5.1   *Conceptual level of phases in survey knowledge-production cycle.*

the client takes place after the data have been constructed. Figure 5.1 shows the conceptual levels appropriate at the main phases in the chronology of a social survey.

Standardisation
Successful interpretation of survey data, at phase 3 in the cycle of survey knowledge production, requires that the data in the matrix should be combined – these separate atoms of knowledge amalgamated to form a picture of the social world as a whole for the client. This kind of collapsing of the matrix can only be meaningful if the entries within each row and each column are comparable. The entries within a single row provide a profile of the case featured in that row – a series of values on variates for this one case. Aggregation of the entries down a column (that is, across cases for a single variate) produces a statistical distribution which can be characterised as to central tendency, dispersion, and so on.

If the profile provided in one row is to make sense, the same case must be measured on all the variates in that row. The case may be an individual person, a grouping of people such as a household or a family, or possibly an inanimate object such as a house, a farm, or a firm. Whatever it is, it must remain the same throughout the row. Examples of a case changing during the sequence of measurements are not hard to find. An informant reporting on her son George may slip at some point in an interview to reporting on her son James. An informant who thinks of his household as consisting only of his immediate family may be taught by the researcher to define the household as including also a couple of lodgers who are allowed to use the family's sitting room. To begin with, in answering questions about the household, he may apply this new definition, but as the interview goes on he may slip back into using his own earlier definition. When the case changes from variate to variate in this way, not only does it become meaningless to compare values obtained on different variates in the row but the measured case may no longer be one of the cases designated for the data matrix; indeed, as would be true of the misdefined household given as an instance above, the measured case may not even be a member of the population of cases being investigated in this survey.

A similar argument applies to the entries in a single column of the data matrix. Here the preservation of comparability is very much harder than in a single row, because each case in the column is likely to be reported upon by a different informant whereas all the entries in one row are likely to come from the reports of just one informant. Moreover, in an interview survey different interviewers are likely to contribute to one column but each row is likely to be produced by the work of a single interviewer. Standardisation down the column, however, requires that the same set of values on the same variate should be applied in every act of measurement intended to produce a datum for that column. The researcher has to take great care to ensure that comparability within each column is attained, and much of the work that goes into the preparation of the mode of measurement for a column is devoted to this difficult task.

Presuppositions about the Social World

An act of measurement can only produce a valid datum if presuppositions made by the client about the other three terms in the survey data model – the social world, the informant and the researcher – turn out to be correct. Before launching into a discussion of the presuppositions about the social world, I should make two things clear. First, all attempts to classify the social world, whether made in a survey or by direct observation of the social world, make these presuppositions. Secondly, the social world is the one element in the survey data model that the researcher is not at liberty to adjust. The first three terms in the model all represent cognisers (Subjects), and the researcher, in his pursuit of valid data, may well have to adjust the cognitions of any of these – including, of course, those of the client, whose knowledge needs may initially be quite impracticable and may have to be changed before the researcher can agree to undertake the survey. If, therefore, the presuppositions about the social world built into the data matrix are disconfirmed, the researcher cannot change the social world to fit the matrix but rather must persuade the client to agree to a change in the matrix.

We need to understand that the crossing of a case with a variate to form a cell of the matrix, although we may think of it as posing a research question ('What is the value of this case on this variate?'), in fact *asserts* far more about the social world than it *asks*. To begin with, it asserts that the case exists (more properly, in terms of our theory of knowledge, that it 'affords information' about itself – for the time being we need not be concerned about whether anyone is around to pick up the information). For illustration, let us imagine that an employment survey is being carried out, and the case is a person. It asserts, further that the variate 'applies' to the case. Let us take 'having an occupation' as our example of the variate. The assertion, therefore, is that our person is a member of the class of persons who have an occupation. The implication of the existence of this one class of persons is that at least one other class can exist – persons other than those who have an occupation. The fact that we are attempting to construct a datum for this cell implies that the person is not a member of the latter class. So far, then, the data matrix cell has asserted that our case exists and is a member of a class (that defined by the variate) which forms part of a classification scheme (consisting, as any classification scheme must, of at least two classes).

We now come to the values on the variate. Each of these also represents a class – a subdivision (or species) of the large class (or genus) defined by the variate. A classification scheme – as used not just in surveys but in all measurement, including measurement of the natural world – is bound by logical laws that go back at least as far as the writings of Aristotle. According to these laws, each case must belong either to the class defined by the variate or to the alternative class and, at the next step of division, if it belongs to the class defined by the variate it must also belong to one, and only one, of the subclasses formed under that. class. Returning to our example, the person either has or does not have an occupation. The fact that we are trying to construct an occupational datum for him means that we are assuming that he must belong to one, and only one, of the occupational groups to which the values on the variate correspond. The classification of occupations prepared for the 1971 UK Census (OPCS, 1970) contained 222 occupational unit groups. The data matrix cell in which a person is assigned to one of these unit groups makes quite a complicated and specific assertion: that this person belongs to a class in a classification scheme which includes at least one other possible class (which may or may not contain any members), that the class he belongs to itself divides into 222 further subclasses and that he belongs to one (only) of these (see Figure 5.2).

The person ...

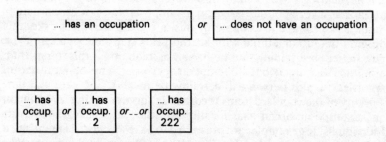

Figure 5.2 *Structure of social world implied when person is assigned to 1971 UK Census occupational classification.*

Generalising, we can say that any data matrix cell makes at a minimum the assertion about the structure of the social world shown in Figure 5.3. In the simplest instance, here portrayed, there is a choice of two possible values to be entered in the data matrix cell. The 'does not apply' category at the preceding step of division may or may not in fact arise depending upon the relationship that exists between the class of cases being surveyed and the class defined by 'variate applies'; if the former class is entirely included in the latter there can be no cases to which the variate does not apply (for example, if persons are measured as to age and every person is presumed to have an age, there will be no entries in the class of 'ageless' persons).

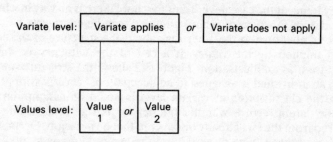

Figure 5.3 *Minimum structure of social world implied by a cell in a data matrix.*

The assertion implied by a data matrix cell about the structure of the social world is in two parts – an assertion about the variate and an assertion about the values. Sometimes the assertion about the variate is based on a datum about the case already constructed and entered as a value in another cell in the row for this case. To the extent that a valid act of measurement was carried out to fill that cell, then, we need not doubt whether the assertion about the variate will be confirmed. But this is not always what we find in surveys. The classification of the case at variate level is often based on assumption and not on an earlier datum. A prominent example of this is when a person is asked his opinion about something without the prior step being taken of the researcher ascertaining that he has an opinion about this thing. If an opinion is assumed but does not in fact exist, any opinion datum recorded for this person will certainly be invalid.

Many of the standard items recorded in surveys are in fact based on an assumption about classification of the case at variate level. Individuals, for example, are presumed to have an age (as I mentioned before), a date and place of birth and a sex. Often they are assumed to have a place of abode and, if over a certain age, to have had an education. Their place of abode is presumed to consist of rooms, and the rooms to have some form of heating. Their education is presumed to have taken place in a school, and so on. My object is not necessarily to query the propriety of these assumptions being made in a specific survey but to point out how much the variates of the data matrix assume about the structure of the social world. It is as though the client has written a book about the social world and the task of the researcher and informant at the data-construction phase is to go through the book filling in gaps in the text. This task can only be carried out successfully if the book gives an accurate account as far as it goes. Even if the informant knows that Jane eats the same breakfast every day, he will not be able to complete the following piece of text: 'On December 32nd Jane had . . . for breakfast'. And, to return to one of our standard survey items, if the case never went to school there is no way in which a valid datum for 'type of school attended' can be constructed.

Let us now turn to the assertions about the structure of the social world implied by the *values* in a cell of the data matrix, taking occupation as an illustration. Figure 5·2 shows the structure implied when an individual is assigned to an occupational classification. Here again the classification at variate level is based on assumption. No specific datum records whether the person 'has an occupation'; it is inferred from the fact already discovered that he has a job. Occupation is taken to mean 'type of work' and the assumption made at variate level, therefore, is that anyone who has a job does some type of work. Work, of course, has many aspects, and for each aspect there is a possible typology that could be made the basis of an occupational classification. These aspects include: the work environment, materials used, end-products, implements used (tools, machines), level of skill required, social status of the work, activities undertaken by the worker. Any of these aspects (or of others that could easily be imagined) might be taken as the basis for defining a 'type of work' variate and the specific types identified would form the values. (For example, if 'type of work environment' was the variate, 'indoors' and 'outdoors' might be the values.)

The aspect of work on which the OPCS *Classification of Occupations 1970* focused was 'the kind of work done and the nature of the operations performed' (OPCS, 1970: vi); in other words, it emphasised activities undertaken by the worker more than any of the other aspects mentioned above. (This aspect is the basis on which most occupational classifications are formed, for example, the US Census classification and the International Standard Classification of Occupations, and it was emphasised still more in the 1980 version of the OPCS classification.) The classification at the values level, then, consists of groupings of activities. What is being asserted about the social world, however, is not just that people can be grouped according to the kinds of activities their jobs entail but that these groups form a logically defined classification scheme: every person with a job must fall into one, and only one, of these 222 groups.

How accurate is this assertion? There are two ways in which it could be inaccurate: first, if a person with a job fell into none of the groups, so that the classification failed to be exhaustive; secondly, if a person with a job fell into more than one of the groups, so that the groups failed to be mutually exclusive. Failures of the classification scheme to be exhaustive do occasionally occur, even when great pains have been taken to ensure that it covers every case. Occupational classifications are updated regularly but the social world does not stand still between the updatings. For instance, the first edition of the CODOT scheme introduced by the Department of Employment, London, in 1972 did not allow adequately for a junior secondary (middle) schoolteacher, a baby sitter, a rigger on an oil rig, or a vending-machine filler – all occupations that developed in Britain in the 1970s with changes in society, in the economy and in patterns of work. Exhaustiveness of a classification can always be guaranteed in a formal way by setting up a 'residual' category, which absorbs all cases falling within the class defined by the variate (or within some broad divisions formed within that class) other than those that can be assigned to the specific categories at values level. The residual category is handy for data construction but often lacks all distinctive character and is so hetero-geneous as to be useless for data interpretation. Plato made this point in the *Statesman* when condemning the practice of dividing mankind into Greeks and barbarians (people who did not speak Greek and sounded – to the Greeks – as though they were saying 'bar-bar-bar'). The latter, he said, was an indeterminate class made up of peoples who had no intercourse with each other. (A further problem with residual categories – that they often present coding difficulties– is covered on pp.117 below).

Failures of the groups to be mutually exclusive occur rather often in occupational classification schemes. People who have any type of work at all often seem to have more than one type of work activity. The *General Report* on the Census of England and Wales of 1861 said that 'double occupations' were a 'great source of difficulty'. The same person might be 'an innkeeper and a farmer; a maltster and a brewer; a fisherman in the season, a farmer or a labourer in the rest of the year' (General Register Office, 1863: 30). Over a hundred years later double occupations are still a source of difficulty. They may take the form of seasonal variation in jobs, or of a person having two jobs throughout the year, or of a single job containing two types of activity. According to CODOT, the last of these forms is increasing in frequency; there is a 'growing trend towards occupational flexibility, typified by workers trained to do two or more previously distinct occupations' (Department of Employment, 1972, Vol. 1:14).

Faced with this problem of a data matrix cell which misrepresents the structure of the social world, occupational classifiers have fallen back on various remedies. All these represent attempts to tackle, in the occupational context, what is really a much more general problem. Occupation defined as type of activity is in fact a behavioural variate, and behaviour has a time dimension – it occurs at some moment in time or over some period of time. Survey researchers tend either to record a highly specific behaviour, often a single action, or to obtain a summary measure intended to represent the behaviour over a long period of time. (The problems that these two approaches cause for informants will be covered in Chapter 7.) The occupational measure is an example of the latter; it is the activities performed day after day for as long as the person has held his present job that define his 'occupation'. And it is the fact that these activities tend to vary over time that poses the problem of how best to represent them with a single value in the matrix cell.

From a data-construction point of view the best solution to the problem of double occupations is to set up a generic category to cover both. For instance, the CODOT scheme, on which the 1980 OPCS classification is based, provides three kinds of generic category for specific combinations of occupations. But setting up generic categories produces a problem of its own: if a new category were established to represent each specific combination of occupations found, the categories would proliferate far beyond what users of the data require and many of the categories would contain very few cases. One restriction that OPCS sets on its occupational unit groups is that each group should usually contain at least 5,000 cases in the UK population. This sort of restriction would immediately rule out most of the combination categories. A way around this is to gather cases with multiple occupations into residual categories. This is, in fact, one of the devices for handling multiple occupations provided by CODOT. The approach guarantees that these cases will be covered by the classification scheme; and, because residual categories are so inclusive, they should have no difficulty in meeting the minimum-size restriction that is likely to rule out many of the specific-combination categories. But this inclusiveness is, of course, their basic weakness; the user has no way of discovering what mixes of occupations the residual categories contain. A solution that makes the construction of data feasible, therefore, may yield results that are useless for data interpretation.

Since generic categories do not supply a complete solution to the problem of cases fitting more than one occupational category, classifiers fall back on selecting one of the (multiple) occupations performed by an individual and classifying him according to that. The problem now is to decide which occupation to use to represent the person's activities. The method employed is to single out some characteristic of the activities themselves or some correlate of these activities and to use this as a device to select one occupation as representative. CODOT says that if a specific-combination generic category does not exist – and I might add parenthetically that experience shows that it often does not – then the case should be assigned to the occupation covering the 'major component' of the work performed. (Only if this fails is a residual category to be used.) But no clue is offered as to how the 'major component' is to be assessed. It might be taken to mean what the person was trained to do, or what he was hired to do, or what he spends most of his work time doing, or what he regards as the most important of his job activities. All these are legitimate interpretations of 'major component' but they are not necessarily correlated with each other and might all lead to different decisions about the categorisation of a particular case. The 1861 Census of England and Wales took importance as the criterion: 'the enumerators were instructed to this effect, that "a person following more than one distinct trade may insert his occupations in the *order of their importance*"; and in the classification the first occupation was generally taken' (General Register Office, 1863: 30). In the 1970 US Census a 'lowest-code' rule was used that could be applied mechanically. All the values had been allocated code numbers, and if the person's job consisted of more than one occupation that with the lowest code number was assigned. According to a post-censual validational study, the effect of this rule on people in the engineering, scientific and technical jobs covered by the study was that some bias occurred – 'fields of specialisation were favoured over managerial functions' (US Bureau of the Census, 1978: 9).

When we allocate a value on an occupational variate to a person we claim to be giving a complete account of that person's type of work (as defined by the variate) – we claim to be measuring all the social world relevant to that data matrix cell. But when the person has more than one occupation the datum can provide only a partial account, measure only part of the relevant social world. The part described may be described accurately but it is less than what the cell claims to be describing. The datum, therefore, fails the test of validity. It is incumbent upon the researcher to make his data for this column in the matrix transparent and thus to enable the user to judge whether these less than valid data suit his purposes or not.

I have now looked in some detail at one instance in which the assertions about the social world implied by the values in the data matrix cell are not confirmed. The problem with the occupational measure is that it claims that each person in a job does one, and only one, of a specified set of types of work. If this claim is correct – and in the majority of cases it seems to be – the survey researcher goes on to claim that by applying an appropriate mode of measurement (a set of procedures involving informant and researcher) he can match person to type of work and construct a valid datum. But if this claim is not correct – and the evidence from 1861 to the present day seems to be that in a number of cases too large to be ignored it is not – then there is no mode of measurement that can save the day; any 'matching' of person to type of work must misrepresent the social world and eventuate in an invalid datum. Can the problem be solved by finding a better set of values? More than one classification of work activities exists, and all seem to share this problem. Or could it be that a little more care in constructing the category definitions is the answer? It seems unlikely. I would venture that more effort and loving attention has been given to the building of occupational classifications in many countries and over many years than to any other survey classifications; if a solution of this kind has not emerged yet, it never will.

Could it be, then, that a different variate would be appropriate – a measure employing a typology of a different aspect of work? Obviously one cannot say that no typology of aspects of work could be found that would match the structure of the social world perfectly. But no such scheme has yet come my way. And it is important to bear in mind that accurate representation of the social world is only one of the requirements for validity that we place on a data matrix; the other is that it should generate data relevant to the knowledge needs of the user of the survey. Not all typologies will necessarily meet the latter requirement.

I suspect that all survey measures, though in varying degrees, make assertions about the social world that prove in practice to be wrong. The kind of analysis applied above to the occupational variate would produce broadly similar results in application to other variates. The root of the problem seems to be that the act of classification presupposes in the material classified a structure that often simply is not there. (This has, of course, been pointed out by many writers before but never, so far as I am aware, in connection specifically with the construction of social survey data.) Classification presupposes a world of similarities and differences, in which like things can be placed in the same class and unlike things in different classes. A world that was flatly homogeneous could not be classified as all its members would belong to the same class, and classification requires a minimum of two classes. But equally a world that consisted entirely of disparate things could not be classified as each thing would have to be assigned to a separate niche, and classification requires the possibility of any one class containing more than one member. Classification presupposes a world of sharp discontinuities; class membership is an all-or-nothing matter, so that things classified together in some respect are entirely, and to an identical degree, members of that class in that respect.

Interestingly enough, perhaps surprisingly, the world we live in does seem to provide a rather good fit to this rigid and abstract classificatory model. The natural world does appear to consist of a small number of distinct building blocks and processes (elements, molecules, atoms, particles, 'fundamental forces', and so on). Among living things we find both sameness and variation, and it is the biological classifications that are always referred to as examples of the use of classification schemes. The social world – the world of people and man-made objects and cultures and institutions that survey researchers attempt to describe – also to a great extent fits the classificatory model. Effective living seems to require effective categorisation, and man not only finds and uses the categories given in nature but imposes his own categories upon nature as he creates his social world. Human reproduction is still a relatively natural process and the birth of a human being is not directly conditioned by man-made geographical boundaries or man-made conventions as to the measurement of time. Yet people born on land seem never to be born in a no-man's land between specific places or with, so to speak, the left foot in one place and the right in another. And, since birth is not instantaneous, some babies must start being born just before midnight and finish just after. By social convention, however, they are not assigned two birthdays, or no birthday. Everybody has one place of birth and one date of birth. Likewise, most people do have only one occupation; society has learned, and taught, that jack of all trades is master of none.

But the account so far has been synchronic – an account of a world which, when held still in time, does show a pattern of similarities and differences. When the time dimension is introduced, the fit of the world to the classificatory model becomes much less good. The classificatory model as established in ancient Greece presupposed a static world. Indeed, its intention was to reveal through categorisation the unchanging realities that lay behind the fleeting forms and super-ficial appearances of the world as immediately perceived. If a thing must be either A or not-A, wholly in one class or wholly in the other, as the model requires, there is no possibility of movement between classes (unless movement occurs altogether outside of time) because, in the process of moving, the thing would have to find itself at some moment between the classes or partly in one and partly in the other. Yet movement, change, seems to be one of the most striking features of the social world – especially of the social world as captured in a survey data matrix, which is pitched at the low conceptual level of everyday life. Survey clients tend to be particularly interested in the most rapidly changing aspects of this rapidly changing social world; it is precisely because of this rapidity of change that the current state is unknown and needs to be measured.

A survey is sometimes likened to a still picture of a moving process. If this likeness is correct, then perhaps a succession of measurements, as taken by a continuous or repeated survey, should produce from the still shots a moving picture of the process like that obtained from 'stroboscopic movement' in the cinema. This may well be what is achieved over a series of surveys but, to continue the analogy, it does not overcome the problem that the picture taken by a single survey is blurred; the shutter speed is too slow. Another much more ancient parallel is contained in Heraclitus's 'you can't step in the same river twice', amended by his follower Cratylus to 'you can't step in the same river once'. Continuing the metaphor, Alexander Pope wrote in his *Epistle to Cobham*: 'Life's stream for Observation will not stay.' It is the dynamic, fluid, fluctuating character of the social world that rebels against the attempts of the static, rigid classificatory model to nail it down. And this is revealed in the fact that a standard survey classifi-cation, such as the occupational classification, not only needs revision every ten years or so but, even at the moment it is created – a 'moment', incidentally, which may well occupy months or even years – fails to provide a perfect reflection of the structure of the social world.

Survey researchers are, of course, not the only people who struggle to classify the social world. Administrators and lawyers devote much of their time to trying to fit a strait-jacket of precise definition on to a slippery substance that in the end always escapes their grasp.

The social world seems, then, in some ways easy to classify and in other ways very difficult: it falls into groups readily enough but groups that lack the absolutely distinct boundaries required of classes in a classification scheme. Some variates divide almost naturally into classes and others do not. The best guideline to researchers is perhaps still the earliest – Plato's explanation in the *Phaedrus* of the method of division: 'The ability to divide a genus into species . . . , observing the natural articulation, not mangling any of the parts, like an unskilful butcher' (Plato, 1973 edn: 82). This instruction to 'cut at the joints' rather than hack through the bone does not mean that in the data-construction phase of a survey we should be attempting to set up what have been known as 'natural', as opposed to 'artificial', classifications. All survey classifications are artificial in the sense that a definite act of selection by the researcher, guided by the knowledge needs of the client, is the starting point for classification. What the researcher selects, moreover, is not necessarily a classification which is scientifically fully adequate (the example usually given of a natural classification is the classification of whales with people, under the heading of 'mammals', rather than with fish, under the heading of 'sea-dwelling creatures'). In survey terms, this sort of adequacy is more likely to be achieved at the genotypic level of data interpretation than at the phenotypic level of data construction. A classification which observes 'the natural articulation' in the data-construction phase is one which requires the informant and the researcher-as-classifier to make only those cognitive discriminations that they are capable of making; and here we must remember that this cognitive work must be at a fairly low conceptual level.

It is useful to think of the data matrix as the set of anticipatory schemata with which the client gains knowledge of the social world cases. The variate and values of each column in the matrix form one such schema. Anticipatory schemata, writes Neisser, 'prepare the perceiver to accept certain kinds of information rather than others' (1976: 20). 'Other information will be ignored or will lead to meaningless results' (ibid.: 55). So far I have said that the data matrix makes assertions about the structure of the social world. More strictly, in terms of our theory of knowledge, the data matrix specifies the kinds of information afforded by the social world that the survey is capable of picking up. If information of these kinds arrives, the presuppositions about the social world made by the data matrix are confirmed and the way is open for valid data to be constructed. (The next question, to be dealt with in Chapters 6 & 7, is whether we have informants who can pick up this information and research staff who can transmit it to the client.) If information of these kinds does not arrive, however, valid data cannot be constructed. An attempt to carry out data construction under these conditions will produce either non-data (entries in the cells that do not purport to be data) or invalid data (purporting to be valid).

Failure of the data matrix to reflect the structure of the social world ranks, in the opinion of the writer, with failure to achieve the conditions for good work by the informant as the two main sources of invalid data in surveys. The two seem frequently to act together: a slight distortion of the social world built into an act of measurement makes it far more likely that the informant will misunderstand the question or will be unable or unmotivated to provide an answer of the kind required. Both problems, of course, must be laid at the door of the researcher. It is his job to devise a matrix that fits the social world and to devise acts of measurement in which the informants are able and willing to play their parts.

Yet failures at data matrix level have been given far less attention in the survey methods literature than deficiencies of the informant. The matter tends to be treated as a 'frame of reference' problem, which confuses two entirely distinct issues – failure of the data matrix to match the social world, on the one hand, and failure of the informant to understand or perform the task the researcher sets him, on the other. A separation of the contributions of the social world (as Object measured) and of the informant (as part of the method of measurement) to the survey datum is needed if failure of the data matrix to fit the structure of the social world is to be seen clearly as the source of invalid data it undoubtably is. A very thoughtful early treatment of the problem is given by Coombs (1953). He analyses the constituents of data into *what is imposed* and *what is discovered* and points out that we must not claim to have discovered what we have imposed. His subject-matter is psychological scaling methods, which he characterises according to their 'searchingness': the most searching discover most and impose least. Ask a person to rank-order three objects and an ordinal scale must result if he co-operates, but set him to make paired-comparison judgements and he may say that A > B, B > C, but C > A – the paired-comparison task, unlike the rank-ordering task, permits intransitivity of judgement to be discovered. My purpose has been to stress, in this research arena far removed from that of Coombs, that much of the character of a survey datum is imposed by the data matrix cell rather than discovered from the informant.

Achieving a Well-Designed Data Matrix

The conditions for the design of a matrix capable of being filled with valid data have now been laid out in some detail. The client has certain needs for knowledge, which dictate the content of the cases, variates and values of the data matrix, and which also dictate the standardised form that these cases, variates and values must take. The social world has a certain content and form, which also must find reflection in the cases, variates and values of the data matrix. And there is a limit to the conceptual level at which the informant and the researcher-as-classifier under normal circumstances can function, which sets restrictions on the conceptual level of the variates and values. In preparing a data matrix, therefore, the client's needs must be set against the properties of the social world, and if the two are in conflict it is the former that must be adjusted. If the two are in harmony but at a conceptual level too high for data construction further adjustments must be made.

Chapters 6 and 7 will cover the conditions that must be satisfied by the work of the informant and of the researcher-as-classifier if valid data are to be constructed. In the limiting case, when a mode of measurement cannot be devised that will allow these conditions to be satisfied, the researcher has to obtain the client's agreement to drop the variates affected from the data matrix. In this limiting case, then, the conditions on the people who classify are also conditions on the design of the matrix. But if the conceptual level at which the data are to be constructed has been kept to the level of everyday thinking, and if the cases, variates and values in the matrix have been matched to the structure of the social world, then this limiting case should be a very rare occurrence.

If we think of the variate and values in one column of the matrix as constituting the cognitive schema which guides and directs the acquisition of knowledge in each cell in that column, then clearly, since items of data are constructed one by one, there must be a cognitive cycle carried out for the filling of each cell: the schema specifies the information appropriate to it, seeks out the information, picks it up and registers it (enters a value in the cell). For each case there is a new cycle, so that in a survey with several thousand cases to be measured there are several thousand cycles. But this cycle is not the complete cognitive cycle as described by Neisser (1976). In ordinary perception the final stage of a cycle is a modification of the schema itself in preparation for the next cycle, and so on. Part of the power of Neisser's theory is that it accounts for both the rigidity and the flexibility of human cognition. But flexibility cannot be permitted in survey measurement once the first datum has been entered in a matrix column. The cognitive cycle has to be aborted at its final stage – or, perhaps more precisely, it can be permitted only to confirm the previous schema, not to revise it. The mode of measurement for a particular column, which permits some variation in the procedures employed from one act of measurement within that column to another, is a device for ensuring that the schema does remain the same for every act of measurement. It attains what perceptual psychologists call 'distal constancy' (in our terms, an accurate picture of the social world) by permitting 'proximal variation' (different images on the retina of the cogniser of the social world).

The requirement for standardisation down the columns of the data matrix, that is, the requirement of a fixed schema for every cell in a given column, has to be reconciled with the requirement for the schema to match the structure of each social world case. Both requirements must be satisfied. To achieve this, as well as the other conditions on the design of the matrix outlined earlier, the researcher undertakes studies of relevant literature, 'thought experiments' and, when necessary, special pre-pilot exploratory studies of the social world of interest to the client. In this preparatory work he goes through cognitive cycles, whether at second hand through his reading, or in his imagination, or in direct first-hand investigations, which may well end in revisions of his schemata. It is useful here to distinguish pre-pilot investigations, whose purpose is to establish the design of the data matrix, from pilot studies conducted after the matrix has been designed as an important step in the construction of appropriate modes of measurement for each of the variates in the matrix.

Although it is conceptually necessary to distinguish steps taken to design the data matrix – the topic of this chapter – from the steps taken to fill the matrix once it has been designed, in the actual practice of a survey the one stage merges into the other. While most of the variates and values are likely to be fully specified before any of the work of data construction commences – we can call them 'pre-classified' – there may be some that are not finally specified until after the researcher has obtained the relevant information from the informants – these may be called 'post-classified'. (These terms should not be confused with 'pre-coding' and 'post-coding'. Coding is not the same as classification – the difference will be elucidated in Chapter 7. Post-classified variates have to be post-coded but a pre-classified variate is not necessarily pre-coded. The major occupational classifications are examples of pre-classified variates that have to be post-coded.) Post-classification takes place in the course of the translation of information into data and must be completed before any case is finally assigned a value. It occurs because the schema for a variate cannot be fully established until the information about a sample of the survey cases has been examined. Perhaps a new region of the social world is being investigated, the structure of which is not known in advance of the survey. This is likely to be true in a study that is itself exploratory and preparing the ground for a quantitative survey of the kind dealt with in this book. But another reason for post-classification, which can apply in a well-prepared quantitative survey, is that if the social world is very rapidly changing in structure a classification set up prior to the survey may be not slightly out of date when the survey is conducted, as the occupational classification is, but entirely out of date. Schuman and Presser (1979) report on the results of a question, asked in the USA, as to what was the 'most important problem facing this country at present'. Their intention was to compare 'open' and 'closed' versions of this question but their findings can also be used to illustrate the hazards of pre-classification. Previous research had indicated that five value categories would absorb almost all the answers: Crime and Violence, Inflation, Unemployment, Quality of Leaders, Breakdown of Morals and Religion. But when the question was asked, the eastern half of the country was experiencing a very severe winter and 22 per cent of the cases were assigned to a category not included among those five: Food and Energy Shortages.

6

The Data-Construction Process I

Chapter 5 dealt with the design of the data matrix; this chapter and the next deal with the filling of a matrix that satisfies the conditions laid out in Chapter 5. When these conditions are achieved we have the possibility of valid data. Whether this possibility is realised depends upon the steps that are taken in the construction of the data.

The data-construction phase of a survey is conducted by the researcher working with the informant. It consists of a process of transmission (and, if necessary, conversion) of knowledge from its everyday form as information in the head of the informant to its classified form as data in the data matrix. If a datum in a particular cell of the data matrix is to be valid it must be *relevant* to the needs for knowledge of the survey client, which means that it must take one of the values on the variate for the column in which that cell occurs, and it must also be *accurate* – the value it takes must correspond to the position of affairs in the social world.

Data Construction as Task Performance

In Chapter 2 (pp. 21–3) a social survey was presented as a three-phase process in which the goal of the first phase was to design a data matrix, the goal of the second was to fill the matrix, and the goal of the third was to draw conclusions from the data – to produce a final knowledge product for the survey client. It is data that are to fill the matrix in the middle phase, and data are items of classified knowledge – knowledge, that is to say, that conforms to the logical laws of a classification scheme. Clearly, the construction of data requires the existence of someone who can put knowledge into a classified form. In the terms of our survey data model this someone must be either the researcher or the informant. At this point it will be useful to divide the researcher function in two and to distinguish the *researcher-as-classifier* (a function performed either by the interviewer, who speaks directly to the informant, or by the office coder, who does not speak to the informant but classifies information obtained by the interviewer from the informant) from the *research director*. The classification of knowledge into datum form is carried out either by the informant or by the researcher-as-classifier (the interviewer or the office coder). The role of the research director in data construction is to set tasks for the informant and for the researcher-as-classifier and to see that they are performed satisfactorily.

There are three basic tasks that the research director sets:

for the *informant*
   either (A) to present an item of classified knowledge – a datum; or (B) to present information (that is, knowledge not yet in classified form);
for the *researcher-as-classifier*
   to work up the information of Type B presented by the informant into the classified form of a datum.

The distinction between the informant's task of Type A and task of Type B is very important and now requires a closer look at the two main types of survey question as they have been traditionally identified. The task set by the research director to the informant often takes the form of a question, and it is usually referred to under that title, but there are two reasons to prefer the use of the word 'task'. First, many survey 'questions' do not end with question marks and therefore are not questions according to everyday usage. 'Enter here your date of birth' is not a question but is identical in its intent to the question 'What is your date of birth?' What they have in common is that they are requests to the informant to provide knowledge about the social world. (Linguists sometimes use the word 'requestion' for this hybrid activity.) As such, they instruct the informant in a task that he is to perform. Secondly, there is a theoretical advantage in treating a survey 'question' as a task. It links the informant's role to that of the researcher-as-classifier and facilitates their comparison. The research director sets tasks for the informant and tasks for the researcher-as-classifier. What are the requirements for successful task performance? How well equipped are they to carry out these tasks? The task approach enables one to relate the activities of the informant and the researcher-as-classifier in social surveys to more general notions of task performance in other walks of life.

Two Main Types of Survey Question

There are many ways of categorising survey questions but one way that is used by almost all writers is to categorise them as either 'open' or 'closed'. It is easy enough to provide typical examples of these two types: 'What was your occupation last week?', followed by a blank space in which the answer is written, illustrates the open question, while 'Are you married, single, widowed, divorced, or separated?', each category being followed by a code symbol to be ringed if the case falls into that category, exemplifies the closed question. But there does not seem to be any generally agreed-upon conceptual definition of open and closed. This may well reflect the lack of a theory of data construction in surveys. A typology of survey questions should serve a theoretical purpose. It should throw light on the problems of data construction and should make discriminations that facilitate the construction of valid data. The open/closed distinction seems to be used more as a shorthand device for talking about questions than as an aid to thinking about them.

Some writers define a closed question as one which presents a set of alternatives explicitly to the informant so that he can select the one that best applies; all other questions then, are open. One consequence of this definition is to treat as open a question which presents explicitly some, but not all, of the possible alternatives. What is probably the commonest type of survey question is therefore defined as open – the 'Yes/No' question. For instance, the question 'Is your child going to school?' states explicitly one alternative ('child going to school') but leaves implicit the other alternative ('child not going to school') and must therefore be an open question. On the other hand, the question 'Is your child going to school or not going to school?' offers both alternatives explicitly and must be closed. This seems unsatisfactory. The two questions are essentially synonymous and would satisfy exactly the same client knowledge need. A useful typology would surely treat them as both of the same type.

In another approach the difference between open and closed is treated as equivalent to the difference between 'post-coded' and 'pre-coded' questions. The distinction between a post-coded question (that is, one to which an answer is given in words, which are converted into a code symbol by an office coder later) and a pre-coded question (that is, one which is assigned a code symbol in the field by the informant or the interviewer) has the virtue of clarity and is of practical importance to the researcher: he must know whether he will need to call on the resources of a coding office as part of his mode of measurement for a given variate. But if 'open v. closed' means exactly the same as 'post-coded v. pre-coded', why use both terminologies? The latter pair of terms is explicit and should suffice. Clear and practical though it may be, however, there are grounds to doubt whether the distinction between post-coded and pre-coded, with its emphasis on where the coding operation is performed, is of theoretical value. It lumps together interviewer coding with informant coding and separates both these from office coding. But the gap between interviewer coding and office coding is much smaller than the gap between interviewer coding and informant coding. Interviewer coding and office coding are both researcher functions carried out by trained experts in social observation. A worthwhile typology would surely group them together and separate them from informant coding.

If *where coded* (office *v*. field) is not a theoretically useful basis for a typology of questions, *by whom coded* (researcher *v*. informant) might seem to be closer to the mark. But a moment's reflection will show that all questions are capable of being coded by the researcher once the informant has supplied the relevant information. For many simple questions it is a purely arbitrary matter and of no theoretical significance whether the questions are asked and coded by an interviewer or presented in writing to the informant and then coded by the informant. Perhaps it would be more useful if, instead of focusing upon the survey-specific coding function as a basis for a typology, we looked at questions as used in everyday life and as analysed by linguists. Can linguistics provide us with any hints as to a more satisfactory typology of questions?

Linguists seem not to make much use of the terms 'open' and 'closed' but they do set up their own typologies, some of which closely parallel the open/closed distinction. (For a sample of linguistic writings about questions see Hiż, ed., 1978.) Quirk (1976) categorised all the interrogatives (over 5,000) that occurred in 130 texts, each of approximately 5,000 words, lodged at the Survey of English Usage. About half these texts consisted of originally written and half of originally spoken material. Some of his categories occur infrequently or never in surveys. These include dependent interrogatives (questions without question marks, sometimes found in surveys, for example, 'Please look at this card and tell me which of these statements best describes your job' or a question beginning 'I would like you to tell me whether . . . '); elliptical versions of 'Yes/No' questions such as 'You going out?' (too colloquial for survey use, liable to set such a relaxed atmosphere that the sense of participating in an important joint task directed by the researcher might be lost); and declarative versions of 'Yes/No' questions uttered either with a rising intonation (for example, 'You are going out?') or with a tag on the end (for example, 'You are going out, aren't you?'), both of which tend to suggest that the questioner expects one answer rather than the other and which therefore are not suitable for use in social surveys. Others of Quirk's categories, however, are often found among survey questions. He divides his non-dependent interrogatives (questions with question marks) into 'Yes/No' questions, 'Alternative' questions (defined as offering the possible answers explicitly) and 'X' questions. 'X' questions were given this name by Otto Jespersen because in them 'we have an unknown quantity x, exactly as in an algebraic equation'. 'X' questions are introduced by what linguists call a 'wh-word' – who, which, what, why, when, where, and so on – and also how. Jespersen contrasted 'X' questions with 'nexus' questions where 'we call in question the combination (nexus) of a subject and a predicate' (Jespersen, 1933: 304–5). Thus 'nexus' questions include both the 'Yes/No' and the 'Alternative' forms of question identified by Quirk.

The 'X' question v. 'nexus' question typology produces something close to the 'open' v. 'closed' typology of survey research but does so in a way which throws into relief the cognitive task that the question answerer has to perform – presenting an 'unknown quantity' as opposed to saying whether a (known) predicate applies to a (known) subject. In fact, the degree to which the quantity is known varies greatly from one 'X' question to another. (Even in algebra there is a limit to the degree to which an x is unknown; at the very least it has to take a numerical, rather than some non-numerical, value.) It might be better to think of a continuum of questions at one end of which would be the totally open question and at the other the totally closed. To the extent the question is phrased at all, of course, it puts some restriction upon the range of legitimate answers, so the totally open question is a contradiction in terms – a question in which nothing is known, not even the question. Unstated questions are encountered, however, and as an illustration of this extreme position on the continuum one can take the psychoanalyst sitting just out of sight of his patient and saying absolutely nothing. He wants a 'free response' and knows that anything he says is likely to contaminate the patient's answer. So the most open question is no question at all; and the same is true of the most closed question where everything is known, including the answer, which may be illustrated by the army sergeant asking for three volunteers – 'You, you and you'.

All questions may be thought of as arrayed somewhere on this continuum between the question in which nothing is known and the question in which everything is known. But if we seek to simplify this structure into a dichotomy, at what point on the continuum is it appropriate to drop our cutting line? From a survey data-construction viewpoint a key theoretical issue is whether the informant, to whom the question is put, is to do the work of classification or simply to present (unclassified) information. It will be recalled that this was the distinction introduced earlier between tasks of Type A and Type B. The ramifications and implications of this distinction will be brought out later. For the moment let us consider the nature of a dividing line drawn in this way and the matter of which questions will fall on either side of this line.

Classification consists of the assignment of a case to a value on a variate. The dividing line on the continuum of questions can be drawn between questions which require the informant to assign the case to a specific value (Type A) and questions which require the informant to present evidence as to the position of the case on the variate but do not convey the specific values (Type B). Type A questions thus include

'Yes/No' and 'Alternative' questions (that is, Jespersen's 'nexus' questions) but also include an important class of 'X' questions in which the values on the variate are not explicitly stated but are so strongly implied as to ensure that what the informant produces is knowledge in a classified form. Examples of this class of 'X' questions are 'What is the date?', 'What is the time?', 'How old are you?', 'What day of the week do you go to the supermarket?', 'What sex is this person?'. These are questions in which there is a single set of values on the variate known by all members of the culture. Researcher and informant are members of the same speech community, and the language on which this community is based provides a standard set of values for the variate, so that once the variate is mentioned the legitimate values are known. Culturally shared category structures are commoner with quantitative variates on which there is a known unit of measurement – that is variates which form interval or ratio scales – than with qualitative variates. But 'day of the week' and 'sex' are instances of culturally shared nominal-level variates. Type B questions include all 'X' questions in which the values are neither stated nor strongly implied.

In applying the A/B typology a definite act of judgement has to be made. Deciding whether a question puts the main burden of classification upon the informant or the interviewer (in an interview survey) is not always easy and obviously there are instances in which the work is shared between informant and interviewer. By contrast, it is very easy to say who does the coding (that is, who enters the code symbol on the survey questionnaire – whether it is the informant, the interviewer, or the office coder) and where the coding is done (in the field or in the office). But these *coding* distinctions do not have any theoretical significance whereas the issue of who is the *classifier* does. Any survey question can be formulated as a Type A, with the burden of classification on the informant's shoulders, and most survey questions can be formulated as Type B, classified by the researcher-as-classifier. The validity of the data depends crucially upon which one is selected, as will be made clear in the discussion of the validation of the data-construction process. For the moment it should be said that there is always a tendency to push too much of the burden of classification on to the informant, just as there is a tendency to require the informant to perform at a higher conceptual level than he is capable of (this point was dwelt on in Chapter 5, pp. 74–5). The result in either case must be a loss of data validity.

While most questions fall into either Type A or Type B, some constitute combinations of both types. For instance, it is common to find a question which specifies values on the variate but, if the case takes a particular value, asks the informant to 'give more details' or to 'explain more fully'. This particular value may well be a residual category. An example is:

'Is Mary at home, at school or somewhere else?'
Home 1
School... 2
Somewhere else (give details) 3
....
....

This question could, of course, be redesigned as two questions, the first as in this example and the second, to be used if the answer 'somewhere else' was given, asking where Mary actually is. Redesigned in this way the typological status of the question becomes entirely clear: it is a Type A question followed by a Type B question. Another combination question type, sometimes found on interviewer questionnaires, is a Type B question with a printed coding frame for use by the interviewer and an instruction to 'prompt as necessary'. Such a question begins life as a Type B but, under certain circumstances ('as necessary'), may be treated as a Type A.

Stages in Data Construction
For each column in the data matrix the research director devises a mode of measurement – a set of operations aimed at ensuring that the goal for that column (that is, the assignment of each case to one value on the variate) is successfully achieved. The principle of standardisation (discussed in Chapter 5, pp. 78–9) requires that the goal should be the same for every cell in a given data matrix column. But the path to the goal, the act of measurement by means of which the goal is reached, may vary from cell to cell. The research director selects whatever path to the goal maximises his chances of constructing an accurate datum. His aim is to combine rigidity in definition of the cases, variates and values of his data matrix – once measurement has begun these cannot be changed – with flexibility in selection of appropriate procedures of measurement. The mode of measurement for a data matrix column consists of the sum total of operations performed in all the acts of measurement employed in dealing with that column. It is this total set of operations that must pass the process-validational test if the data in that column are to be regarded as valid.

The process of data construction takes place in three main sequential stages dominated respectively by the research director, the informant and the researcher-as-classifier.

(1)   In the first stage the research director selects the informants for the survey and formulates a standard knowledge-provision task for

them. The task will either be of Type A (to *classify* the social world) or of Type B (to *provide evidence about* the social world), as described already.

(2) Once the informants have been selected and their task, usually in the form of a written question, has been formulated, the second stage can begin. Here the informant enters the survey for the first time (although much of the preparatory work up to this point will have been executed in anticipation of his entrance). The task is now presented to the informant. Some process of comprehension of the task must take place, followed by task performance. Analytically it is useful to see the performance as consisting of two steps: first, retrieval of knowledge (the bringing to bear of the relevant cognitive schemata); then, presentation of the task outcome, the cognitive product, to the research director. The presentation of the task to the informant by the research director and of the task outcome to the research director by the informant may be made by word of mouth or in writing. The key issue for quality of data is whether the research director (in the person of an interviewer) is present during the second stage of the data-construction process. If the research director is present he can, if need be, adjust the act of measurement in such a way as to produce a valid datum. If the research director is not present there is obviously no way in which he can intervene. At the end of the second stage the informant presents his task product to the research director; the informant's role in the survey is now completed.

(3) The cognitive product presented by the informant as the outcome of his task may be either *a datum* or *evidence* about the social world. If the product is a datum, all that remains for the research director to do at the third stage is to enter the datum in the data matrix cell. If the product is evidence, however, the researcher-as-classifier now appears for the first time in the survey. The research director sets as a task for him the assignment of the case to one value on the variate on the basis of the evidence provided by the informant. The researcher-as-classifier performs this task and presents the task outcome to the research director, who enters it as a datum in the matrix cell.

Performance of the Data-Construction Tasks

Data construction consists of the performance of tasks by the informant and (sometimes) the researcher-as-classifier that are set them by the research director. Any time person Z is set a task by person Y there are certain conditions that must be satisfied if the work of Z is to please Y. First, Z must *understand* just what it is that Y wants him to do. This is an indispensable precondition for successful task performance. Next, Z must be *capable* of performing the task and *willing* to perform it: whatever resources are needed must be made available to him and whatever stimulus is required to motivate him to perform the task must be supplied. Y attempts to achieve these conditions through the selection of an appropriate Z, through giving him whatever background training may be needed, through instructing him in how to perform the specific task and through supervising his performance of it.

The purpose of this simple – I hope not simplistic – analysis of the task performance of one person working on behalf of another, given in rather general terms, is to prepare the ground for a discussion of task performance by the informant and the researcher-as-classifier in the process of data construction. For any mode of measurement the research director has to take the key decision as to whether the task for the informant should be of Type A (classification) or Type B (provision of evidence), and this decision must hinge on his assessment of the degree to which the conditions of understanding, ability and willingness are met respectively by the informant and by the researcher-as-classifier. If he decides in favour of a Type B task he must then take another key decision – whether (in an interview survey) it should be the interviewer or the office coder who classifies the social world according to the evidence provided. (This issue is discussed below on pp. 127–9.) Whichever task he sets, the research director must wrestle with the problem of ensuring that the data-construction personnel fully understand what they have to do and are able and willing to do it. Pilot studies are almost always required in order to explore ways of satisfying these conditions and to test whether they have in fact been established. This book is not the appropriate vehicle in which to carry a detailed account of methods of pre-testing (whether in the form of pre-pilot tests of the design of the data matrix or pilot tests of the design of modes of measurement) but an attempt is made here to indicate what the *goals* of pre-tests should be.

There are important differences between the informant and the researcher-as-classifier in what is required of them and their capacity to supply it. Both of them have to classify the social world but the informant, in addition, must know the social world and be able to retrieve this knowledge and present it as evidence – attributes not required of the researcher-as-classifier. But the difference which has the most far-reaching implications takes us back to the basic character of informant and researcher as laid out in Chapter 2. The informant is not an expert, professional observer of the social world whereas the researcher is. Informants are non-standard, varying greatly in the degree to which they meet the conditions of understanding, ability and willingness. The research director selects the informant for the survey but in practice has very little power of choice; there is often only one person who possesses the knowledge of the social world that is the fundamental requirement of any informant. For some variates it may be useful to ask the informant to check records or to consult with other members of his household to supplement his own unaided memory, but much of the time the research director has simply to accept the informant with whatever limitations he has. Almost by definition of the informant as non-expert, background (pre-survey) training is not given to him. To some extent, however, it is possible for the research director to vary the task-specific instructions and supervision that he gives the informant. The informant task itself consists of a standard instruction given to all informants. In an interview survey – though not in the absence of an interviewer when an informant himself completes a form – the research director in the person of the interviewer is able to intervene in an act of measurement to compensate for a failure of the conditions of understanding, ability, or willingness to be satisfied. Cannell and his associates (Cannell, Oksenberg and Converse, eds, 1979; Oksenberg, 1978) have reported some fascinating and theoretically very important attempts at gaining research control over the process of instructing and supervising survey informants and at making sure that the process serves the aim of construction of valid data.

By comparison with the non-expert, non-standard informants, whose task performance often has to be assisted by the research director through his special intervention in an act of measurement, the researcher-as-classifier is an expert performer of his task. As a paid worker in the survey organisation he will have been selected, at least in part, for his capacity to perform the classificatory task and will have been given the background training needed to make him an accredited expert in the observation of the social world. As an expert he should be on a level of equality in task performance with his colleagues; they should be functionally interchangeable, all meeting in a standard way the requirements of understanding, ability and willingness. In order to ensure that this level of performance is maintained a set of standard supervisory procedures will be put into effect by the survey organisation, but there should be no need for any special intervention by the research director in an act of measurement at this third stage in the data-construction process. The intervention at the second stage is carried out because the conditions of understanding, ability, or willingness fail. At the third stage no compensatory intervention should be needed, as the conditions should never fail.

Conditions on Good Work by the Informant

Before discussing the three conditions, of understanding, ability and willingness, that must be satisfied if the informant is to perform his task in the data-construction process well, a few points need to be made clear. First, informant error is entirely the responsibility of the researcher. Sometimes discussions of informant error almost give the impression that the researcher conducted his side of the survey impeccably only for the informants to let him down. The entire interaction of informant with researcher takes place on the researcher's initiative. The conditions on good work by the informant are all capable of being manipulated by the researcher who selects, instructs and supervises the informant with the aim of securing good data. If he succeeds he should take the credit, and if he fails the blame. Secondly, if by his selection of informants alone he can ensure that the three conditions are satisfied for every mode of measurement in the survey, the obvious course of action is for the researcher to conduct his survey by post and to eliminate the role of the interviewer. But if, for any one act of measurement in the survey, the intervention of the research director is needed to enable any of the three conditions to be satisfied, an interviewer will be required. Thirdly, because informants are non-standard, the degree to which the conditions are satisfied when the informant is selected and the consequent degree of need for an interviewer's intervention may vary greatly as we move from one cell to another within the same data matrix column. The researcher has to ensure that the conditions are eventually satisfied for every act of measurement in the matrix.

When the three conditions have been considered, one by one, we shall return to the question of the decision between informant tasks of Types A and B.

Understanding

The first condition for successful task performance by the informant is that he must understand the task he is set – that is, take it to be what the researcher intends it to be. In dealing with this condition we confront at once the problem of language.

The informant speaks the language of everyday life when he talks about the social world as defined by the knowledge needs of the client. The researcher, however, speaks a rather different language when dealing with this social world – a language of technical terms, sometimes using the same words as those of the everyday language but giving these words special non-everyday definitions. The reason for the difference is that the everyday language is the language of information whereas the technical language is the language of data. Everyday language, as part of its function to organise thinking and aid communication, groups the objects and events of the social world and to this extent assists the researcher in his aim of setting up categories on his data matrix variates. But its groups tend not to be classes in the sense required for a classification scheme obeying the strict logical laws, and to this extent it hinders the researcher. Common nouns, for example, define categories but these categories often have fuzzy boundaries. In a survey we need to know in precisely which of a set of categories a case falls and this can only be achieved if each category is clearly delimited from every other one. The difficulties that follow for informants when their task is to classify the social world will be covered on pages 111–12 below.

For the time being we need to recognise the problem that the researcher confronts in conveying understanding of the task to the informant when he is compelled to use the language of everyday life. Clearly, it is that language rather than the researcher's language that must be used. The researcher moves into the informant's territory – literally in that he may be taking an interview in the informant's own home and metaphorically in that the inquiry is about the informant's personal life space – and he must obey the elementary traveller's law: when in Rome do as the Romans, that is, speak the language of the natives. This language, which is the medium of data construction, the means of communication between researcher and informant in their joint work of constructing the survey data, just as it both aids and hinders the conversion of information into datum also both aids and hinders the researcher in his conveying of their task to the informants. He begins with the great advantage that he and all his informants (this discussion will not cover the special, exceedingly difficult problems of surveys that cross language barriers) are members of the same speech community defined by their sharing of what Saussure (1916) called a common *langue*. It is this fact which provides the basic guarantee of standardisation down each column of the data matrix that was mentioned in Chapter 5 (p.79) as one of the conditions that the design of the matrix had to satisfy. It is likely that a different informant assists in the construction of each datum in the column; yet, because of the shared *langue*, it is possible for the researcher to formulate a single task for every act of measurement in that column.

But the possession of a common *langue* does not mean that all members of the speech community will necessarily construe the social world in an identical manner. I have pointed already to the special technical language that the researcher has to develop for his own survey purpose. Lyons writes: 'It is by no means clear that the language spoken by all the members of a given speech community is as uniform, and structurally determinate, as Saussure assumed' (1970: 15) and 'In the last resort, we should have to admit that every member of every speech community speaks a slightly different dialect: he has his own *idiolect*' (ibid.: 19, italics in original). Idiolects are not the only source of potential misunderstandings between the researcher and the informant. *La langue* itself, because it groups into fuzzy-edged categories rather than classifying precisely, impedes the clear conveying of meaning. It would be out of place in this book to become involved in a discussion of the relationships between language, thought and the world. But there seems little doubt that language, whatever its origins, functions as a cognitive model placed upon the world and facilitates thinking about the world and the communication of thoughts between people. The social world develops and changes, and language, because it avoids a rigidly logical classificatory structure, affords an adequate model of that world. At an everyday level, the everyday language works. One feature of this language is polysemy (the possession by the same word of two or more meanings), described by Ullmann as 'in all probability a semantic universal inherent in the fundamental structure of language' without which there would be no metaphors and language would 'be robbed of much of its expressiveness and flexibility' (1963: 183). What works in general, everyday use, however, does not work for the survey researcher trying to convey a standard task to all his survey informants. There seem to be two main sources of misunderstanding of which the researcher has to beware.

(1)   There are words or sentence structures that entirely defeat the informant's comprehension – words that convey no meaning at all or sentence structures that are so complicated as to be uninterpretable. The researcher needs to bear in mind that his own vocabulary is likely to be fuller than that of his informants and that, in particular, his technical vocabulary is not likely to mean anything to them. It may be difficult to disentangle the meaning from sentences containing multiple negatives, and the researcher should be aware that, for people answering No to a Yes/No question, even a single negative in the question produces a double negative in the total meaning unit consisting of question and answer. Implied negatives are as great a danger as the more obvious no's, nots and nevers. Two examples I have recently noticed are, from the *Guardian* of 17 January 1978, 'It would be idle to deny that there have not been differences between Boycott and others in the party on this tour', which seems to contain one negative too many (or too few), and Bradburn, Sudman *et al*. 'Few people would argue that no one falsely disclaims illegal or contranormative behavior in an interview situation' (1979: 86) which contains only one explicit negative but at least five that are implied, not to mention the word 'argue', which can mean either 'maintain' or its opposite, 'dispute'. A common trap for the researcher in formulating a task for the informant is to try to add to the clarity of the task by hedging it about with qualifying clauses. Because he seeks a precision that the everyday language cannot readily attain his pursuit of clarity leads only to confusion. An example would be a question about a person's hours of work containing subclauses telling the informant how to treat travel time, meal times, other breaks in work, paid overtime and unpaid overtime.

(2)   The cases just mentioned were all instances of the task for the informant being meaningful to the researcher but meaningless to the

informant. An equally potent source of misunderstanding is when the task means one thing to the researcher but something different to the informant. One way in which this comes about is through the ambiguity which is such a pervasive feature of language. Payne (1951) listed 1,000 'frequent-familiar' words, based on a count of words occurring most frequently in popular American magazines and reading words known by 9-year-old American children, and then devoted a chapter (ch. 10) to an analysis of the problem words occurring in this list – words presenting problems, that is to say, to the writer of survey questions. One word to which he drew attention was 'you', which may be taken as either singular (you the individual) or plural (you the household, or family, or work group, or community, and so on). According to Payne, 'you' was the twelfth most common word in American magazine writing. From a count made by the author, however, it is the word used more often than any other in survey questions; and 'your' is the sixth most common. All the questions asked in forty-nine recent surveys conducted by the OPCS, covering a very wide range of subject-matter, were listed and a count was made of the words occurring in every twenty-fifth question. The twenty most frequently found words were, in order: you, the, to, or, of, your, in, for, a/an (the two forms treated as one word), do, have, did, what, any, not, how, it, would, that, is. ('It' and 'would' were tied in frequency.) The word that took fourteenth place, 'any', is another standard source of ambiguity. Payne points out that the meaning of the question 'Do you think any word is better than the one we are discussing?' depends on how 'any word' is interpreted. One and the same person might answer 'No' if he takes it to mean 'any old word' or 'Yes' if he takes it to mean 'at least one word'.

Much misunderstanding that takes the form of words being interpreted differently by the researcher, on the one hand, and the informant, on the other, arises from the researcher's attempt to use everyday words but with a special 'data' meaning. In talking about the informant's living arrangements, for example, the researcher may use words such as 'household', 'rooms', or 'building' that he defines carefully (to himself) in order to meet the demands of logically based classification schemes. Every case in a survey of individuals may be defined as belonging to one, and only one, household; every piece of living space must be defined as either constituting a room or not constituting a room; rooms are found in buildings, and a clearly defined conceptual boundary must be set up between one building and the next. In the course of making these definitions, the researcher is very likely to depart from the everyday usage of the very people who belong to these households and occupy these rooms and buildings. In this situation he has various possible solutions to the problem of establishing mutual comprehension between himself and his informant. He may simply avoid the use of these ambiguous terms, but this means he must find alternative words that serve his purposes better – which may well be impossible. He may try to teach all his informants his own definitions by building them into preambles to the standard survey task; or he may introduce his definitions selectively when he feels an intervention by the research director is needed to correct a misunderstanding on the part of the informant. The likely deleterious consequences of trying to teach informants elaborate classificatory rules will be returned to when we take up the issue of deciding between Type A and Type B forms of task. For the moment we should be aware that these solutions to the problem of ambiguity may create a still greater problem of total meaninglessness for the informant as definition is piled upon definition.

Ability

Given that the informant understands his task to be what the researcher intends it to be, the next condition for good work by the informant is that he should be able to perform it. We can distinguish three challenges to the informant's ability that any information-provision task sets. First, the informant must have, at some time, obtained knowledge of the social world under investigation; it is his presumed possession of this knowledge, of course, that led him to be selected as an informant. Next, he must be able to retrieve this knowledge. Informant tasks vary greatly in the demands they place upon memory, but all of them require, in some degree, the retrieval of stored knowledge. Finally, he must be able to present the knowledge retrieved in the form required by the researcher. Here is where the main difference between the tasks of Types A and B arises.

(1) One of the requirements outlined in Chapter 5 for the design of a data matrix capable of being filled with valid data was that the social world should afford information of the kind specified by the cells of the matrix. But information afforded is not necessarily picked up. The selection as informant of a person who has picked up the information afforded is really the fundamental precondition for good work by informants. Except in the special conditions of a record-keeping survey or of a mode of measurement in which the informant looks up a document or asks another member of the family for information, survey data are based on knowledge acquired by the informant before the survey and independently of it. How much choice of informant the research director has depends greatly on the social world area under study. If the case to be measured is a social group or institution the researcher may be able to choose which of several possible informants is likely to know the social world best. In a survey of rented property it might be the tenant or the landlord; in an employment survey it might be the worker, the shop steward, the foreman, or the employer. If the

case is an individual, although this person may be the obvious first-choice informant about himself – not true always, for example, if the person is senile, deaf, or a non-speaker of the language in which the survey is conducted – the information the researcher requires may be possessed by his spouse or another family member.

(2) Even if an informant for an act of measurement has known the social world item specified in the data matrix cell the issue still arises of whether he can retrieve it from memory. Some surveys seek quite detailed records of recent events; others seek histories, complete with dates and durations, of aspects of people's lives – their jobs, housing, education, or health, their pregnancies and childbirths, their children's lives so far. In discussing the problems these surveys pose we do not have access to a well-established theory of memory. The position here is no stronger than in cognitive psychology generally. However, there are several factors that are widely agreed to affect memory and there is a large body of work on the problems of memory in social surveys (for example, Sudman and Bradburn, 1974: ch. 3; Moss and Goldstein, eds, 1979; Sudman, 1980). The problems of remembering events that occurred in a specific period of time are, first, the tendency to forget (that is, to omit items that should have been included) and, secondly, the tendency to 'telescope' into the period events that in fact occurred outside it (that is, to include items that should have been omitted). (The term 'telescope' has been used differently by different writers – some to mean drawing events more distant in time into the recall period, by analogy with the telescope as a viewing instrument, and others to mean bringing into the recall period events that occurred on either side of it by analogy with the telescope as a concertina-like collapsing instrument. Dictionary makers seem only to admit the latter meaning.) I shall touch briefly first on what the researcher can do to counteract forgetting, and then on a technique designed to prevent telescoping.

Events best recalled by those who participated in them are those that occurred most recently, those that are salient or distinctive, standing out from other events in the person's life, and those that the person has had other occasion to rehearse. These factors, unfortunately, cannot be manipulated by the research director in the act of measurement: recency and sálience are characteristics of the social world event outside the researcher's control, and 'other' rehearsal occurs independently of the survey by definition. Two techniques do, however, seem to be of proved effectiveness in aiding informants' memories. One, which requires skilled intervention by an interviewer, consists of linking the event about which recollection is sought (as it might be, the date on which a new job was started) to a salient event that occurred at about the same time (say, a holiday or the birth of a child). The other takes advantage of the superiority, well known to psychologists (for example, Klatzky, 1980: ch. 10), of recognition over recall: an experimental subject who looks at a list of words and later is asked either to produce the words from memory (*recall* task) or to identify them on a new list containing the words first seen scattered among many other words (*recognition* task) performs much better on the latter task. The memory of a survey informant should likewise be improved if categories are explicitly presented orally or in writing ('prompted' is the term often used) rather than being left implicit or entirely unindicated.

The solution to the problem of telescoping is to obtain a record of events that took place just outside the specific period of interest to the client and to use this as a check on events reported as occurring within that period. The approach was developed by Neter and Waksberg (1964); an extension of it is described by Sudman (1980).

Every act of measurement presupposes that the informant possesses the item of knowledge inquired about – that it registered on him originally and now may be successfully retrieved. Sometimes this assumption is tested with a 'knowledge' question – 'Do you know (the answer to question Q)?' – and those who say 'Yes' are then asked question Q. Much more often the knowledge question is omitted and question Q is asked directly. The assumption that the informant knows the answer to a survey question is as sweeping in its own way as the assumption (discussed in Chapter 5, pp. 79–90) that the social world has the structure attributed to it by the data matrix cell. No doubt the social world has characteristics that are well known to almost all potential survey informants but researchers may be overambitious in some of the knowledge that they attribute to informants. One of the standard problem areas of data construction that has received much attention in the literature since Lazarsfeld's classic paper (1935) is the use of the question 'Why?' usually asking informants the reasons for their own or other people's actions. Such a question presupposes, first, that people have reasons for their actions (that is, that the social world has the structure that the data matrix cell asserts) and, then, that they know what these reasons are. Even if the former presupposition is true, the latter may not be. For practical purposes a survey is restricted to obtaining information that can be summoned up using standard survey questioning practices. The researcher is neither a psycho-analyst nor a police-station interrogator. In deciding what he may legitimately expect from his informant and what method to pursue to get it, the survey researcher interested in asking 'Why' questions would do well to look at the parallel attack on the problem made by social psychologists in the last two decades under the label of 'attrib-ution theory'. What the studies in attribution theory have in common, according to Wimer and Kelley, is 'a concern with laypeople's causal explanations for the occurrence of events in their lives' (1982: 1142).

Acquaintance with this work would at least alert researchers to the formidably difficult tasks that 'Why' questions pose to informants.

(3)   A person may know the social world in a way satisfactory for everyday purposes – that is to say, he may have picked up information afforded by the social world and may be able to retrieve it – but he may still have great difficulty in converting this information into the form in which the researcher wants it presented. The researcher wants it either in the form of a classified datum (product of Type A task) or in the form of information (product of Type B task). If a Type B task is set, there should be no great difficulty for the informant at this stage. Assuming that pick-up and retrieval have occurred successfully the information should be readily available for presentation as evidence on the basis of which the researcher-as-classifier can form a datum. Difficulties for the informant arise when a Type A task is set.

A task of Type A may seem easy enough when the social world falls neatly into classes and *la langue* recognises this by giving each class a name. Where everyday knowledge is already categorised the level of information may seem to be the level of datum. But even in this situation the categories given in the language of everyday life may not form classes in the strict logical sense. The ambiguity in language, that was described as a hindrance to clear communication in the discussion of the problem of achieving understanding above, is also a hindrance to classification by use of words. Just as the social world bursts the logical straitjacket in which classification tries to bind it, so language, through such devices as polysemy and change in meaning over time, defies the rigid constraints of the Aristotelian system. The word 'bird', for example, broadened as a semantic category in its development from the Anglo-Saxon 'brid', which meant simply 'young bird'; while the word 'fowl', which used to denote all birds, now for most purposes is restricted to the barnyard variety (Ullmann, 1962: 229, 231). Eleanor Rosch (1978), in a series of brilliantly conceived experiments on the categorisation by people of observable objects from the world around them (as opposed to categorising tasks carried out on specially pre-pared stimuli), has found that their category members tend to bear a 'family resemblance' to one another rather than all sharing a common attribute or set of attributes as the logic of classification would require. Each category is organised around a prototypical concept or instance and its members fall on a gradient of degree of prototypicality, some being closer to the prototype than others. She illustrates this process with the category 'bird'. A robin, she finds, is the prototypical bird; a hen falls in the bird category but is at some distance from the prototype – a robin, it seems, is a more birdlike bird than a hen. Whereas classification requires that membership of a category should be all-or-none, therefore, members of everyday categories vary in how repre-sentative they are of the category. And whereas classification requires a clear demarcation between categories, the boundaries of everyday categories are fuzzy and indistinct.

Is this mode of categorisation confined to the categorisation of observable things? Rosch (1978, pp. 43–6) has focused her experimental attention on the categorisation of concrete objects but has sketched out a treatment of events using the same approach. Mischel and his associates (for example, Mischel, 1979) have found the Rosch approach productive when applied to people's everyday categorisation of personality types. It seems very probable that Rosch's findings can be extended to all forms of categorising by ordinary people, including the categorisation of the social world by informants in social surveys. One conclusion from Rosch's work for surveys must be that the researcher who sets his informants a classificatory, Type A task may be walking into a minefield. Fools rush in; the prudent researcher will walk as delicately as Agag (but, one hopes, with greater success than that unfortunate Old Testament monarch).

The task of classification becomes even harder for the informant when *la langue* does not provide him with simply named categories, perhaps because the social world does not fall so readily into classes, or when the categories provided by *la langue* are not those that the researcher needs at data level. Problems for *understanding* that we encounter in these situations have already been covered. The problem for *ability* is that the informant is now required to carry out quite a complicated intellectual task if he is to classify the social world. He has to be taught, perhaps, an entirely new concept surrounded by several limiting definitions, any or all of which have to be put into effect when a case is allocated to a category on a variate. Or he has to be taught to discard a concept that has served him very well in his daily existence and to apply instead a variant of it that may seem pointless to him and that necessarily 'goes against the grain'.

Willingness

Good work by the informant requires not only that he should understand his task and be able to perform it but that he should be willing to perform it. What are the motivational conditions needed if the informant is to make his contribution to the data-construction process, and how can they be achieved?

We need to begin by adopting a perspective different from that taken by some workers in this field who seem to have an almost morbid fear of being told lies by their informants. The issue is not how to prevent them telling lies but rather how to avoid putting them into a position in which they are unable to tell the truth. The social interaction between a researcher and an informant is a special case of a very common encounter between two strangers in which one asks the other for information. The normal result of such an encounter is that the person asked gives the information requested. If he fails to do so the reason is very likely to be that one of the conditions already described in this chapter or the last has not been satisfied. If I ask someone the whereabouts of the post office and there is no post office in this place, I am attributing a characteristic to the world that it does not possess and my interlocutor will not be able to supply the information I asked for. Equally, if he fails to understand my question or does not know the answer, my request will not be met. But if these conditions are satisfied I can expect an accurate answer. To be told a lie in these circumstances is memorable because it is salient and salient because it is so unusual.

There are, however, two special features of some survey requests for knowledge that do increase the likelihood of lack of co-operation from informants. (This discussion will not cover the general problem of refusal by selected informants to take part in surveys as that problem is one of data interpretation rather than of data construction. The focus here will be on factors affecting the performance during an act of measurement of an informant who has agreed to take part in the survey.) One is when the informant is asked to tell the researcher something that may lead to a definite injury to himself. The other is when we demand hard work from the informant in the data-construction operation. Both these features, of course, make the survey request for knowledge something altogether different from the request to a bystander to tell one the way to the post office.

(1)   Much methodological effort in recent years, especially in the USA, has been put into devising techniques for persuading informants to provide the researcher with 'threatening', 'embarrassing', 'sensitive' – in other words, with potentially discreditable – information about themselves. Barton (1958), in a research note distinctive for its brevity as well as its wit, applied eight techniques commonly used in asking embarrassing questions to the question, 'Did you kill your wife?' The techniques included the 'Casual Approach: "Do you happen to have murdered your wife?"'; the 'Sealed Ballot Technique' in which the informant was to put his reply in a sealed envelope and 'drop it in a box conspicuously labelled "Sealed Ballot Box" carried by the interviewer'; and the 'Kinsey Technique' (named after the well-known sex researcher): 'Stare firmly into the respondent's eyes and ask in simple, clearcut language such as that to which the respondent is accustomed, and with an air of assuming that everyone has done everything, "Did you ever kill your wife?"' The most fashionable current technique, not invented when Barton wrote, is the 'randomised response technique' (Warner, 1965) in which the throw of a die determines which of two questions (one embarrassing, the other not) the informant will answer, the interviewer being kept in the dark. Probability methods are then used to estimate the overall pattern of

response. This reduces the act of measurement almost to the level of a parlour game.

There is no evidence that these techniques succeed in extracting good information from informants. It has been known for a long time that the survey method fails when informants are asked to reveal discreditable facts about themselves. In an early study Hyman (1944) asked 'Do they tell the truth?' and had to conclude that in three surveys, conducted by a US government department during the Second World War, they did not. The topics inquired about were the selling of war bonds, display of government posters and absenteeism from work. The behaviours reported by informants were compared with official records and the comparison revealed a high level of misreporting. As Hyman says, 'the questions dealt with behavior to which high prestige is attached' (1944: 557) – selling war bonds, failing to display the posters and being absent from work were activities harmful to the war effort. In these rather extreme cases it is hard to imagine that any trick of questioning would have succeeded with every informant.

To try to find ways of manipulating informants into revealing information of this kind seems to me not just unproductive and diversionary, when so much other work aimed at improving data-construction techniques waits to be done, but actively misguided. The informant is an indispensable source of privileged information who should be treated with respect by the researcher. Informant and researcher collaborate as equals in the construction of survey data and there has to be a direct and open relationship between them. If deceit enters the relationship on one side, distrust will surely enter it on the other. To exert pressure upon the informant unfairly or to presume upon his co-operation can only sour the relationship that exists between researcher and informant, to the eventual general detriment of survey data. The researcher has to accept, and to convince the client to accept, that, while some areas of the social world cannot be investigated in surveys because they are not known to informants, others are out of bounds because the quality of information is likely to be suspect. Pre-tests should soon reveal which these areas are and methods other than the survey method must be used to explore them.

(2)   We do not presume upon the informant's goodwill when we ask him to work hard in the construction of survey data. The thesis of this book is that good survey data *can* be constructed, but their construction is difficult and requires a good deal of effort by both researcher and informant. The researcher's effort goes into the creation of an act of measurement that serves the client's need for knowledge and that sets the informant a task within his capacity to perform. He has a right, then, to demand from the informant the effort needed to contribute to a good datum rather than a bad one. The

evidence from recent research, especially by Cannell and colleagues (see Cannell, Oksenberg and Converse, eds, 1979), is that if the researcher makes the right approach the informant will make this effort. (The methods used might also be described as manipulative, but I suspect that they leave a very different taste in the mouth of the informant – a sense of anxiety and of negative feelings towards the researcher after a 'sensitive questions' survey but a sense of accomplishment and of respect for the researcher after an interview in which the informant worked hard to construct good data.)

The Cannell approach has been to depart from the traditional definition of an interview as a 'conversation with a purpose' (Bingham and Moore, 1959: 3). It is a task-oriented activity that must be carried out in a businesslike and professional manner. 'Rapport' is not the aim; a warm relationship between interviewer and informant is no guarantee of good quality data. Indeed, one of the turning-points in Cannell's research was his discovery that positive feedback was as likely to be given by an interviewer when the informant was refusing to co-operate as when he was co-operating. The methods Cannell has introduced of 'commitment' (a formal undertaking to provide accurate information given by the informant before the interview starts), 'instructions' (given by the researcher about the goal of a question and how it may best be reached) and 'feedback' (from the researcher indicating how closely the informant has approached this goal) are all designed to motivate and train and guide the informant in the completion of a rather difficult but achievable task. Whether these methods are going to be applicable in detail in most surveys is neither here nor there – the aim they have is absolutely right.

The Decision between Tasks A and B

Now that we have run through the conditions for good work by the informant we can return to the basic issue in designing a mode of measurement of whether the informant is to do the work of classifying (Type A task) or to provide evidence so the researcher may do the classifying (Type B task). A starting point, which must weigh heavily with researcher and client, is that whereas the researcher-as-classifier is a paid professional the informant is an amateur and usually unpaid. A task of Type A, which cuts out the classifying function of the researcher, is bound to be cheaper than a task of Type B. On cost grounds alone, therefore, Type A must be preferred. In addition, since the Type B task is likely to take at least as long for the informant to complete as Type A, if not longer, and since for Type B a further phase in data construction is required after the informant's task is finished, Type B must be more time-consuming. So on grounds of timeliness as well as cost Type A wins. How do the two types compare on grounds of validity?

The claim is sometimes made for Type A tasks that in removing the researcher-as-classifier (whether in the guise of interviewer or office coder) they remove a known source of error. What is not said is that this known, because measurable, source of error is then replaced by a usually unknown, because unmeasurable, source of error – that of the informant as classifier. In fact, the informant's contribution to error, because of his amateur status as a social observer, is almost certain to be greater than that of the researcher-as-classifier. It is also said sometimes that Type A tasks are better because they are easier for interviewers to handle. But they are only easier for interviewers because the burden of data construction has been passed partly to the question formulator and partly to the informant. The total effort of constructing a datum is not affected by the question type: irrespective of how the effort is distributed, there is still a case to be assigned to a value on a variate.

Considering the two types of task in general, there seems no reason why one should pose greater problems of *understanding* or *willingness* than the other. The main difference is in regard to *ability*. Type A, to the extent that it either states or implies answer categories, makes the retrieval task one of recognition rather than recall and therefore must certainly aid the informant's memory. However, when Type A brings the values on the variate to the attention of the informant it has to do so in such a way that they can be applied relevantly and accurately by every informant. This means that they must be defined clearly, and the informant must be taught the rules governing their use. But the application of a complex set of definitional rules may be beyond the capacity of the informant. While a Type A task, then, may make the remembering of the social world easier it may saddle the informant with too taxing an intellectual demand. We can, and should, expect an informant to work hard on the construction of a datum but the task must be one that he is capable of performing. The Type B task may test the informant's memory severely but it is much more modest in what it demands of him intellectually. It passes this burden on to the researcher. The research director now has to put the task to the informant and to assist him in satisfying the conditions for good work, all the time judging whether he has obtained sufficient information to enable the researcher-as-classifier to apply the definitional rules and assign the case to one of the values on the variate. The problems of a Type B task will be explored in detail later when we are discussing the researcher-as-classifier. For the moment let us consider more closely the intellectual problem posed by a Type A task.

The definitions of the values must be conveyed to all the informants. This means that they must be built into the standard task as formulated for all informants – the written question. They cannot be left in an interview survey for the interviewer to introduce at her discretion in her intervention in an act of measurement. What this would presuppose is that every time the informant was diverging in his interpretation of the task from what the researcher intended he would be aware of this and would draw it to the interviewer's attention. This might happen in extreme cases, for instance when the task seems meaningless to the informant, but would not happen in lesser cases, in which the informant would simply make his own personal interpretation of the task and perform it in the light of this interpretation.

The requirement for a Type A task is that the values on the variate should be capable of being defined simply. This means that the definitions should be brief and they should be few in number. Dealing first with brevity of definition, a value ideally should be defined by one word – the title of a category. A category in a coding frame for use by office coders often has to contain four elements: a title, an explanation of that title running to sentence length, some typical examples of category members, and a listing of borderline cases included in the fringe of the category. The only one of these that should be needed in a value definition in a Type A task is the title. If anything beyond that is needed, the definition is too complex.

One type of category that always presents definitional problems is a residual category in a nominal scale. Since categories on a nominal scale are different from each other but no principle of order governs their arrangement on the scale, each category may border on each other one; so the definition of a particular category may need to specify its difference from each of the others. This problem becomes acute with a residual category, which may have to mop up cases falling just outside the boundaries of several of the other categories. Rather than attempt to make a positive definition of a residual category on a nominal scale, which would be a very complicated task, it is usually given a brief negative definition ('all others' or 'not elsewhere classified'). Such a definition is extremely hard to apply, and even experienced office coders using more highly specified coding frames tend to differ from one another in their use of residual categories (Kalton and Stowell, 1979). This type of category is certainly to be avoided in a Type A task.

It is sometimes said that the number of categories in a Type A task should be limited (perhaps to 5). This indeed applies if the categories form a nominal scale, since each additional category means at least one additional definition and therefore an increase in the complexity of the task, but may not apply if the categories form an ordered series, especially if the series is based on a standard unit of measurement. For instance, it would not be difficult to classify a case as to age in years on a scale from 0 to 120.

Type A, therefore, though desirable because it reduces the cost and speeds up the process of a survey and because it assists the informant's memory, is only applicable when the social world falls into categories that approximate a logical classification scheme and when this structure is represented in the everyday language of the survey informants. A further restriction is that Type A can only be used when the variate is pre-classified. Pre-classification is only possible when the structure of the social world is relatively fixed – that is, values will not appear and disappear between the formulation and the performance of the informant's task – and is known to the researcher when he formulates the task. These conditions, of the social world structure being *stable* and *known in advance*, are only likely to obtain when that structure *does* approximate a classification scheme and *is* embodied in language.

7

The Data-Construction Process II

Classification by the Researcher

When the decision has been taken that the informant's task in a mode of measurement will be of Type B, the research director has to prepare a task for the researcher-as-classifier. This task, to be performed in the third stage of the data-construction process, is typically not presented in the form of a question. The research director instructs the researcher-as-classifier to assign a case to a value on a variate using the evidence that the informant has supplied. The instruction consists of a coding frame to which may be attached a set of rules about how the coding frame is to be used. In this section we shall consider first the nature of a coding frame; then the nature of a coder (a role played by the researcher-as-classifier); next the conditions of understanding, ability and willingness, and how these apply to the work of the coder; and finally how the decision is made on any given Type B mode of measurement as to whether an interviewer in the field or an office coder should perform the coding task.

Nature of a Coding Frame

A coding frame may consist simply of one classification scheme but often contains more than one. A classification scheme, in the strict logical sense of the term, has to be exhaustive and its categories have to be mutually exclusive and formed on a single principle of division (*fundamentum divisionis*). A coding frame may contain several variates from the data matrix, each representing a different principle of division, and the coding operation then consists of assigning the case to a value on each of these variates. An example of this is the structure of a multicoded frame for a 'Why' question shown in Figure 7.1. In this frame the first step is to assign *reasons for leaving a job* (the cases for this classification exercise) to a classification scheme for such reasons. Every possible reason for leaving a job is covered and no reason can fall into more than one category of reasons. These reason categories now become the variates for the survey data matrix. At the next step *people* (our survey cases) whom the data matrix asserts, no doubt on evidence already discovered, to have left a job are assigned to one of the two values ('Yes' or 'No') on the first reason category ('hated the boss'), then to one of the two values on the next reason category, and so on until all the reason categories have been covered for all the survey cases. All the cases must be assigned either to 'Yes' or to 'No' on each variate; in this way exhaustiveness and mutual exclusivity are achieved. They are achieved, of course, at the cost of a massive assumption: that the informant for the case has reported *every* attribute of the case; therefore any attribute *not* reported is not possessed by the case. This interpretation of codes not assigned, which is inescapable in the use of data from a multicoded frame, is an obvious weakness of such a frame.

Figure 7.2 shows a more common instance of a coding frame structure consisting of two classification schemes. Only a single data matrix variate is represented. At the first step in division the cases are separated into a dichotomy according to the quality of the information obtained. Those of poor quality are assigned a code signifying this, and these are the cases for which the outcome of the mode of measurement is defined as being a 'non-datum'. Those of good quality are then divided in the next step of division according to the values on the variate in the data matrix.

Presentation of a Coding Frame Category

A category representing a data matrix value, when presented in a coding frame, has to achieve two things: it must be relevant, genuinely reflecting the matrix value as required by the client, and it must be capable of being used by the coder in such a way as to preserve the accuracy of the informant's evidence. It has, therefore, a dual use – a use to the client, or any other user, in aiding his understanding of how the data have been constructed and what they mean, and a use to the coder in performing his coding task. Logicians have traditionally distinguished the *connotation* of a class, that is, the attributes which any individual member of the class must have, from its *denotation*, that is, the individual members of the class (for example, Mellone, 1945; Stebbing, 1952). For a user to understand the meaning of his data the connotation is needed: simply to be given a listing of the members of the class is not much help. For a coder to apply a frame it is the denotation that is most useful. Looking up each individual in some comprehensive listing is much easier than having to judge whether a conceptual definition applies to it. In practice, it is rare for a survey coder to have access to the complete denotation of the categories in a coding frame; an example would be a directory of employers each of whom has been assigned to an industrial classification, so that once the case's employer has been discovered all that remains is for the coder to look the employer up in the directory and read off the industrial category. Coding frames usually try to present both the connotation and at least

Informant's task: to answer the question 'Why did you leave your last job?'

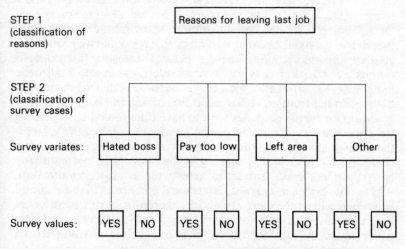

Figure 7.1 *Illustration of the structure of a multi-coded coding frame.*

some instances of the denotation of each category. The four elements in the presentation of a category have been referred to already on page 117 above. They will now be covered in more detail.

(1) The *title*, usually consisting of a single word or a very short phrase, is mainly for use when the survey results are presented to their eventual users. A title ideally represents all the specific meanings embraced within the category but this ideal situation is only likely to

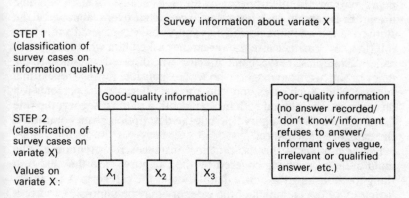

Figure 7.2 *Structure of a single-coded coding frame with a non-data category.*

obtain if the everyday language recognises this 'cut' of the social world. When this ideal situation does apply to all the categories in a coding frame we have, of course, a situation appropriate for a Type A informant task. Often it applies to some, but not all, of the categories. Occupation provides a good illustration. Many jobs, especially those that are well established and well known, have occupation titles that give a complete account of an occupational category (for example, toolmaker, bus driver, typist, computer programmer). If all occupations were so straightforward they could be classified by the informant and coded from an alphabetical list. Many, in fact, lack definite titles and for survey purposes have to have titles forced upon them by the researcher so that a label can be attached to each of the values in the data matrix. Since these titles have to be short they cannot represent all the meanings covered by the category. A common error by an untrained coder is to try to code by use of a category title only.

(2)   The *explanation* gives a conceptual account of all the meanings contained within the category and is, therefore, a statement of the logical connotation of the category. Its purpose is both for use by the coder (unless the full denotation of the category is given), and to serve the client or other user of the data as an amplification or exegesis of the category title. An explanation is obviously necessary if the title does not fully cover the meanings included in the category but can also provide a useful supplement to the title for the coder when the title does cover the whole of the category. For instance, when an interviewer asks an informant for evidence as to his job she asks first what the job is called and then for a description of it. If the job is fully described by its title then the purpose of the job description is not to aid in finding the appropriate code – the title is sufficient for that – but to provide a check on the accuracy of the title: does it conform to what the person actually does or has he, in response to the request for a name, borrowed a title from some other job because his has none? The literature is replete with instances of apparent over-claiming for the status of a job when the person may simply have concocted a title for a job that has none because the researcher asked him what his job was called. Examples are the 'bank director' who directed customers to the teller or the 'traffic manager' who was responsible for the trolleys in a supermarket. Such cases only come to light because the person's job description is compared with the explanation of the category; the title given matches the category title but the description given contradicts the category explanation.

(3)   *Examples* – that is, practical instances representing all the main areas of meaning covered by the category – are the next best thing to publishing the entire denotation of the category. A complete listing of all the members of the category may be impossible, since it assumes that the membership is finite and known, and is almost always

impracticable because of the size of the list. The British *Classification of Occupations 1970* (OPCS, 1970) included an alphabetical index of occupation titles containing over 20,000 entries, but this did not constitute the denotation of the classification if we think of the cases being classified as individual persons with jobs: each occupation title itself formed a category containing a number of people with jobs.

(4)   *Border-line cases*, like examples, are members of the denotation of the category; but where the examples illustrate the central tendency or tendencies of the category, the borderline cases illustrate the boundaries around the category. The explanation includes a conceptual definition of the boundary and the borderline cases consist of practical instances to fill out the definition. If the boundary is not carefully drawn coders are likely to make their own interpretation of how literally to take the definition offered in the explanation, some tending to be 'inclusive' and others 'exclusive'. (The difference may relate to the psychological dimension of 'broad' *v.* 'narrow' categorising – for example, see Pettigrew, 1958.) Cannell, Lawson and Hausser noticed these tendencies in the coding of interviewer behaviour but it can also arise in the coding of the social world by survey coders. They used the terms 'stringency', 'severity' and 'rigor' to describe the variable (Cannell, Lawson and Hausser, 1975: 19–20). The purpose of providing firm rules about boundary cases is to control it.

The Coder (in Field or Office)
The coder's task in an act of measurement is to allocate one code on the basis of the evidence contained in the informant's performance of his task. Depending on the task set in this particular mode of measurement, he may allocate a code signifying that the evidence is not of good-enough quality to permit the assignment of the case to a value on the variate or he may allocate a code assigning the case to a value on the variate. Before turning to the conditions that must be satisfied by the work of the coder if the data are to be validly constructed, let us consider the nature of a coder.

The coder is a member of the same speech community as the informant and, like the informant, has an everyday knowledge of the social world. He has no special subject-matter expertise – that is, he has no special knowledge of some subpart of the social world – but is an expert in the observation of the social world (which, of course, he does not observe at first hand but through the eyes of the informant) and can turn his hand to the observation of any subpart of it that is required. Skill in expert observation means simply the ability to follow a set of complicated instructions incorporated in a coding frame and to apply them to the evidence supplied by informants. The research director selects his coders in such a way as to ensure that they can acquire this skill and then trains them in it. The standard operating procedures of the survey organisation also include various checks and controls as means of verifying that the coders perform their tasks in the skilled way required.

Since the skill of the coder comes down to a precise following of a complex set of instructions it might seem that a machine could do this job better than a human being. Not only is special knowledge of the social world not required, it may actively interfere with a literal following of the coding instructions. The coder should not be too well informed about the subject-matter of the survey; nor should he be too imaginative in his approach. The qualities needed by a coder may seem like qualities that a machine could have. Especially when a variate has been pre-classified and is to be used in a standard way on many surveys it would seem that a machine could be programmed to follow the coding instructions. In fact the evidence so far suggests that machine coding only works if the exact words used by an informant can be matched with a category in the machine. And since this is most likely to occur with a Type A task, all the machine does is to code – not to classify.

There are apparently two reasons why a human coder is indispensable. One is that, as a speaker of the everyday language like the informant, he keeps up with changes in contemporary idiom. As the social world changes so language, as a model of the social world, changes also and unless the computer is frequently reprogrammed it will not be able to take account of these changes. The other, more fundamental, is that the computer lacks the everyday knowledge of the coder who can apply his knowledge of the social world to sort out semantic and syntactic ambiguities in the informant's evidence. The problem is very like that of machine translation (for example, see Bott, 1970). A casual follower of English football has no difficulty in interpreting sports headlines like 'Queen leaves Palace', 'Forest set to sign grasshopper' or 'Yorath plays with injured toe' but a computer, possessing what Miller (1978) calls 'lexical' rather than 'practical' knowledge, might well misinterpret them. In daily life people say things like 'I'm going to shut the door but I'm not going to *shut* it'. On a hospital survey an informant said 'If they'd done earlier they let them in earlier'. The three plural pronouns referred to three different groups of people but the coder had no difficulty in realising that the answer meant that if the patients had finished being washed the nurses let the visitors in before the official visiting time. One can picture a patient who is aware of this arrangement murmuring with Macbeth 'If it were done when 'tis done, then 'twere well/It were done quickly . . .' which, like the informant's answer, would surely baffle a computer.

The coder, then, can do what a machine can and an informant cannot – follow correctly a complex set of classificatory instructions –

and can do what a machine cannot and an informant can – have everyday knowledge of language and of the social world.

Conditions on Good Work by the Coder

Since the coder is hired and trained specifically to do his coding task and since he works in an environment which includes standard control procedures, good work by the coder should be much easier to achieve than good work by the informant. As a member of the survey organisation – that is, as part of the total 'researcher' function – he should have no difficulty in communicating with the research director about the task. If, therefore, there is a problem of *understanding* the frame and any associated coding instructions, this problem should be speedily resolved. As to *ability*, the coder is not required to know the social world or to retrieve knowledge of it in the way that the informant has to. For the coder the ability problem is the problem of matching a survey answer, the evidence obtained from the informant, to a coding frame.

This is perhaps the central problem of the entire process of data construction. The relatively easy areas of the social world that fall naturally into categories given titles in the everyday language have data constructed for them by means of Type A tasks. The Type B task is reserved for the more difficult areas. If all the data-construction procedures have gone well, by the time the coding stage is reached the client's knowledge needs will have been translated into a data matrix and the columns in the matrix will have had modes of measurement established for them. Each mode of measurement for a Type B task includes an informant task (a survey question) and a coder task (a coding frame). If the informant task has been well performed we have an *accurate* answer – evidence about the social world; and if the coder task has been well designed we have a *relevant* coding frame. Successful coding combines the accuracy of the answer with the relevance of the frame to produce a valid datum and, in this way, finally bridges the gap between client and social world that caused the survey to be initiated. Often at this last stage of data construction there is a hiccup in the process. The whole enterprise hinges on the quality of the information extracted from the informant, and this information depends not only on the conditions for good work by the informant being satisfied but also on the research director setting the informant a relevant task. The setting of the informant task includes both the formulation of the standard task (the printed question) for all inform-ants and the way in which the task is presented to the informant (including any probing or subsidiary questioning carried out by the interviewer). Often the information obtained, though accurate enough, is not relevant to the frame; it does not enable the complex set of definitional rules, of which the frame consists, to be applied.

Poor-quality information, then, can arise either because the conditions for good work by the informant were not satisfied or because the task that in practice was set the informant was not relevant to the requirements of the data matrix.

The ability problem that the coder confronts is the problem of how to cope with information of too poor a quality to permit the case to be assigned one of the data matrix values. There seem to be basically three ways in which the problem is handled in practice. One is to assign a non-data code, as was illustrated in Figure 7.2. This has the merit that it amounts to an open admission of defeat; the non-datum is transparent. It is, of course, unsatisfactory from the data-interpretation point of view: a cell in the matrix has to be left blank as an 'item non-response'; in a sample survey it constitutes a failure of the sample achieved to reach the target set in the sample design and to this degree threatens the validity of any conclusions to be reached from the survey about a parent population. In the other two ways of handling poor-quality information the case is assigned a data matrix value based partly on whatever inadequate information is available and partly on assumption. Both these ways, then, opt for the construction of invalid data. Where the ways differ is that one makes the assignment public and the other does not. The term 'by fiat measurement' has been used to refer to the arbitrary allocation of a case to a category (Cicourel, 1964; before him Torgerson, 1958; before him Hempel, 1952). We might call the public version 'classification by fiat' and the non-public version 'coding by fiat'.

Classification by fiat is illustrated by the practice of assigning arbitrary codes to certain poorly described occupations in the OPCS *Classification of Occupations 1970*. For instance, different types of 'turner' belong to different occupational unit groups but if a person is described simply as a 'turner' the convention is that he should be assigned to a particular one of these groups – that for 'metal turners'. The same approach is taken to 'electrical engineers', 'draughtsmen' and numerous other occupations. The practice is made necessary by the fact that the classification was set up principally to code occupation information from the Population Census, and census information on occupation, being filled in by the informant, is generally less adequate than that recorded by an interviewer. Classification by fiat makes the procedure for handling inadequate information public but does not reveal on how many occasions it has to be used. One might describe its data, therefore, as semi-transparent.

Classification by fiat is a source of bias in data: the category to which the convention directs the poor-quality information is likely to be relatively overstocked while some of the other categories are likely to be, collectively, correspondingly understocked. The user of the data will be aware of the possibility of this bias but will not know its extent.

In the case of coding by fiat, the user will know neither of the possibility nor of its extent. A good survey organisation tries to ensure that it does not happen. Any new coding decisions that have to be made after the coding frame has been set up are taken centrally by the research director, are incorporated into the frame as amendments and are made public along with the rest of the coder task. If necessary, cases already coded are recoded in the light of the amended frame.

Willingness as a condition on the good task performance of coders can be dealt with quickly. The basic motivation to perform should be assured by their conditions of employment in the survey organisation. The quality of coders' work should be maintained at a high level by the standard operating procedures of the survey organisation. Whereas informants are selected for their knowledge of the social world – and their possession of an ability to put definitional rules into effect, is, so to speak, a free bonus for the researcher– coders are selected in part for this ability to apply rules. To this original ability the survey organisation adds a learned competence acquired from background training. And the coders may be specially briefed orally and in writing and then tested on the operation of each mode of measurement. Finally, a system of checks and supervision is put into effect so that any falling-off from high standards of task performance can be quickly detected and put right.

The Decision between Field Coding and Office Coding

In some ways the choice between the interviewer working in the field – say, interviewing at the informant's home or workplace – and the office coder working in the central coding unit of the survey organisation is parallel to the choice between classification by the informant and by the researcher-as-classifier. (In contrasting field interviewer coding and central office coding I am looking at extremes on a continuum. For instance, coding by a telephone interviewer permits a much higher level of supervisory control than field coding, and coding done at home by a coder working alone permits much less supervisory control than central office coding.) The starting point again is that one has an advantage over the other for reasons that have nothing to do with quality of data. Field coding, while unlikely to be cheaper than office coding since the coding part of each act of measurement must take at least as long in the field as in the office, is probably time-saving overall in that the work is spread over a very much larger number of coders.

How is the quality of the data constructed in these two ways likely to compare? It is often claimed that interviewers coding in the field have two advantages – they can take account of information that is unrecorded and therefore not available in the office, and they can use the printed category definitions to guide their probe questions. The first of these is as likely to be a source of miscoding as of increased accuracy; a good interviewer should always record any relevant information so that it is as available to the office coder as to the interviewer herself. The second advantage certainly may reduce the incidence of answers that do not match the coding frame but there is no reason why, if the variate is pre-classified, the office coder should not enjoy this advantage also. A good interviewer should be trained thoroughly in the category structure of the variate she is measuring irrespective of whether coding is to be done in the field or the office.

Office coding has a number of very definite advantages over field coding in the quality of the data constructed. It is, of course, the only approach that can be taken with a post-classified variate. With a pre-classified variate it has the advantage that the office coder is both selected and trained to be a coding specialist, whereas the interviewer is principally a research director responsible for finding informants, persuading them to co-operate and intervening in the act of measurement to help them meet the conditions for good task performance; she is only secondarily a coder. The office coder works in a much more favourable coding environment than the field coder. The field coder has to work in what may be distracting conditions and, since she sees only her own small batch of interviews, may only just have learned the coding frame when the coding task comes to an end. The office coder works in conditions in which it is easier to concentrate and, since he handles a much larger amount of work, can learn the coding frame and establish his coding approach on a first group of questionnaires and can then carry this approach throughout the full batch of work.

But the main difference is that with field coding the codes assigned are the product of the individual interviewer alone. Her work is almost incapable of being checked unless a special exercise is mounted – an expensive and therefore rare occurrence – and she has very little opportunity of consulting her supervisor if in doubt about a coding decision. By contrast, in a well-conducted coding office the codes assigned are the product of the coding unit – not of the individual coder. The coding supervisor sits in the office and all coding queries – that is, answers about which the coder feels some doubt as to the correct coding decision – are referred to him. The coders are trained not to make guesses and their work is thoroughly checked. The result is that very little variation between coders occurs.

There is a long tradition of research on interviewer variance (by which is meant field coder variance – it is not variation in interviewers' playing of the role of research director that is investigated). More recently, the literature on office coder variance has started to grow. Experimental studies, paralleling those on interviewer variance, have been made of the coding decisions made by office coders working alone and independently of one another. These studies (for example,

Kalton and Stowell, 1979) reveal, not surprisingly, that when office coders are required for experimental purposes to work as unsupervised individuals they vary in their coding decisions just as unsupervised field coders do. The unwary may be led to conclude that office coding, therefore, has no advantages over field coding. What this conclusion overlooks is that the standard operating situation for the field coder is to work as an unsupervised individual, whereas the standard operating situation for the office coder in a well-run survey organisation is to work as part of a tightly supervised coding unit. The aspect of office coding that needs most attention is the final coding decision that emerges from the coding unit – not the decisions of the individual coders before the supervisory procedures are brought into play. The coding supervisor must ensure that the final decision is consistent with the category definitions in the coding frame. And if he is compelled to make arbitrary coding assignments, he must be sure to attach the rules he applies as amendments to the coding frame and thus to make them instances of classification by fiat rather than of coding by fiat.

In conclusion, from a data quality point of view and when a choice exists between field and office coding, office coding is usually to be preferred – in particular when the evidence from the informants poses complicated coding decisions.

Opinions and Behaviours

At the end of Chapter 2 I argued that opinions do not differ fundamentally from other survey data. Every survey question asks – either directly or, more often, implicitly – for the informant to report his state of knowledge about something. Whether the state of knowledge or the 'something' is taken as the social world element for this question depends upon the client's needs that the question is hoping to satisfy. If the state of knowledge of the informant is the topic of interest, the question is defined as an opinion question; if the 'something' that the informant knows is the topic, the question is defined as one of fact. In Chapter 2 I proposed to divide the social world into an 'internal' part (including opinions and other states presumed to exist within an individual) and an 'external' part (to include everything else), and I promised to take up the problems of constructing opinion data in the present chapter.

The social world is in a continual state of change. In Chapter 5 it was pointed out that for this reason there is often an uneasy fit between the logical model of classification, which presupposes an unchanging subject-matter, and the social world. But some parts of the social world change more rapidly than others and therefore present greater difficulties to the social observer. We can distinguish, for instance, in the social world of individuals *fixed* variates (that is, variates on which values taken by individuals virtually never change), such as sex, date of birth, country of birth, father's occupation and school-leaving age; variates on which values taken *change rarely*, such as person's own occupation, industry, accommodation type, tenure of accommodation, academic qualifications, and marital status; and variates on which values taken may *change frequently*, such as opinions and behaviours. (See the distinction made by Galtung, 1967: 30 ff. between 'permanent' and 'temporal' values.) Opinions and behaviours, no doubt precisely because they change so frequently, are often the main focus of interest in social surveys, where they tend to be analysed by the less changeable background variates. Opinions are, of course, part of the 'internal' social world and behaviours part of the 'external' social world. They pose rather different problems for the survey researcher, and some of these will now be examined.

Let us look first at their modes of change and then at their patterns of co-occurrence. An expression of opinion is best seen as a function of a schema – a state of readiness in regard to the topic of the opinion which guides the expression of opinion and which, like a cognitive schema, may be changed in some degree by every relevant input that the person receives. An opinion's mode of change is therefore continuous, wavelike. An opinion neither has an end nor, usually, a detectable beginning; it has a present existence but no clearly marked chronological history. And, just as there is no reason to set a limit to the number of anticipatory cognitive schemata that can coexist in a single human being, so the number of opinions, or potentialities to express an opinion response, that can occur at the same time in the same person is presumably limitless. Behaviours, unlike opinions, do seem to have definite beginnings and ends. Far from being wavelike – to continue the analogy from physics – they are particle-like; far from being continuous, they are discrete. They are located in time as well as in space. Moreover, there is a definite limit to the number of behaviours that can be performed simultaneously by the same person. He may be able to rub his stomach and pat his head at the same time but, unless he is a contortionist, he cannot also scratch the small of his back. While opinions can exist concurrently, behaviours seem to occur consecutively.

These different characteristics of opinions and behaviours have definite consequences for the ways they are measured in social surveys. It is always past rather than present behaviour that is measured. A behaviour question may be phrased in the present tense (for example, 'What is your usual method of travel to work?'), but it asks about events that took place before the asking of the survey question. The informant's behaviour while the question is being asked, that is, during the middle stage of the data-construction phase of the survey, is *listening to the question and preparing an answer*. Should he also be twiddling his fingers or putting on a kettle, the survey client is almost certainly not going to be interested; and in an interview survey such activities are better recorded as data of direct observation by the interviewer. Opinions, on the other hand, tend to be measured at the present; it is the state of the schema at the moment of expression of the opinion that is measured. This is not to say that it may not sometimes be legitimate to instruct an informant to cast his mind back to some definite past occasion and to ask him about the state of his internal social world at that time but it is a process fraught with danger from the data-construction point of view. The opinion given is very likely to reflect the current state of the schema rather than the state of the schema on this earlier occasion.

Behaviours
Problems in constructing behaviour data seem mostly to flow from the fact that it is *past* behaviour that is measured. We can look, one by one, at the conditions that need to be satisfied if good work is to be done by the informant in reporting behaviour. *Understanding* should not present any special problems. Behaviour, as part of the external social world, is observed by people generally and encoded in the everyday language. Because there is an external referent to the words used to denote it, meanings are likely to be widely shared within the speech community. If behaviours of an 'embarrassing' or 'threatening' nature are excluded from surveys, *willingness* should be achieved without much difficulty. The condition that is hardest to achieve is *ability*. While his own behaviour is presumably always known to the person who performs it, it may not be known at all to a substitute or proxy informant. And even if it has been known to the informant, there may be great difficulty in retrieving and presenting the knowledge in the form required for the survey client.

One problem for the informant in providing information from memory about behaviour deserves special attention. Survey clients tend to want either detailed reporting of specific behaviours, such as the purchase of a single tin of sardines, or a report on some characteristic of a large distribution of repeated behaviours such as a 'usual' or 'main' behaviour. (Occupation was given as an instance of the latter in Chapter 5, see p. 84). It may well be that both of these forms of reporting constitute a departure from the informant's everyday, habitual way of cognising the social world. Rosch (1978) has distinguished a 'basic' level of cognising from a more specific 'subordinate' level and a more general 'superordinate' level. The basic level is the level of everyday cognitive activity. Applying Rosch's analysis to the task of the survey informant, the reporting of individual instances of behaviour seems to require the reporter to operate at the subordinate level, while reporting a characteristic of an extensive distribution of repeated behaviours seems to require him to work at the superordinate level. If we ask a person what he had for breakfast two weeks ago last Thursday he might well have difficulty in remembering. If, instead, we asked about some unique (non-repeated) event in his life that took place on that day, the event might well be salient and memorable and easily reported. It is the repetitive nature of the event that makes a particular breakfast hard to recall. Of course, if his breakfast habits follow a regular pattern (breakfast on Thursdays always consisting of kidneys and mushrooms, let us say) there should be no difficulty. It is pulling from memory a single instance of a repeated behaviour that follows no exact periodic pattern which causes the problem when we try to make informants operate at the subordinate level in Rosch's scheme. One solution to this problem is to conduct a record-keeping survey, but this brings its own problems at the data-interpretation stage, as was described in Chapter 2 (pp. 30–1). The other approach often taken on surveys would be to ask the person what he usually has for breakfast. This approach presupposes that the distribution of values on this variate has a single peak – that is, that such a thing as a usual breakfast exists for the person – rather than being, say, bimodal or rectangular. But even if a usual breakfast does exist for the person there may still be formidable problems in obtaining an accurate report of it. How long back is he to think? At what point in time is this distribution of repeated behaviours to begin? It is surprising how often survey questions in this format give no guidance as to the starting date of the series of events that the reporting is to cover. Suppose it is set to a year ago; suppose also the task is made quite clear to the informant so that he knows what the legitimate values on the variate are. The task may still be a difficult one, calling for quite a complex exercise in descriptive statistics by the informant. He may forget that his winter diet differs from his summer one or that there was a long period last autumn when bacon was in short supply in his local shops. Probably much easier than either the report on a single instance or the 'usual' behaviour calculated over a year is a summary value based on a short period, perhaps two weeks or a month, up to the date of the survey. This last task seems to correspond to Rosch's 'basic' level where the other two represent the 'subordinate' and the 'superordinate' respectively.

Opinions

Because statements of opinion are functions of continuously developing schemata they seem frequently to confront the problem that arises when the static model of Aristotelian classification is applied to a dynamic social world. Let us suppose that a person is to be allocated one of two values on an opinion variate, say, being 'for' or 'against' the United Nations. It may be that while at some past moment he was a strong supporter of the United Nations, at present he feels that the United Nations is an irrelevant, unimportant organisation. He is not against it, but he is not for it either. He does not fall into the class of persons defined by the variate. Alternatively, it may be that the variate does apply to him but his sympathies are shifting from favouring to opposing the United Nations. He is no longer 'for' but he is not yet 'against'. In both these supposed situations a datum cannot be constructed because a presupposition about the social world implied by the data matrix turns out to be incorrect.

Just as was done with behaviours, we can examine in turn the conditions that must be satisfied if good work is to be done by the informant in reporting opinions. Since opinions, as part of the internal social world, lack external referents that can be pointed to and are totally embodied in language, there seems to be much less in the way of shared meanings within the speech community than is the case with behaviours. In this area idiolects seem to flourish and there is always a possibility of ambiguity in the interpretation of the informant's task – different informants taking it to mean different things. *Understanding*, therefore, is likely to pose problems for the researcher. There is no reason to expect *willingness* to present great difficulties. And, unlike in the case of behaviour, opinions are usually only asked of the people holding them – proxy informants are not used – and no memory problems should arise when opinions held at this moment are the subject of inquiry; there should not be any lack of *ability*, therefore, on the part of opinion informants.

It is sometimes suggested that opinion data are of a lesser breed than factual data – less validatable and less valid. On the issue of validity I have argued in Chapter 3 that, in practice, while there may be no valid standard values against which to measure opinion data there are also no valid standard values against which to measure most factual data. And, as to the validity of these two types of data, if we move *faute de mieux* from validation against standard values to a process validational approach there seems little to choose between behavioural data – taking them as one manifestation of factual data – and opinion data. Behavioural data confront special problems of ability of the informant to carry out his task; opinion data confront special problems of his understanding of his task. Each set of problems must be solved if data are to be successfully constructed but neither set is inherently insoluble. From a data-construction point of view there is no special reason to challenge the validity of opinion data.

Arguments against opinion data include the one that opinions are often found not to be consistent with behaviour – a person does one thing and tells us that he thinks another; or that opinions are not responsible, in the sense that their holder is not called upon in life to act upon them; or that a person's opinions are unstable and ephemeral, changing from day to day. All these arguments may be true but they do not cast doubt upon the validity of opinion data. An opinion may be in contradiction with the behaviour of the person holding it, or with others of his opinions, but it may still be a genuine reflection of his opinion schema. All that this goes to show is that the person can tolerate inconsistencies in his life; there is no psychological law that demands total consistency among a person's thoughts or between his thoughts and his actions. Again, a person may hold a genuine opinion about a matter without ever finding he needs to act in relation to it. And the fact that his opinion changes does not mean that, at the moment it was measured, it was not accurately represented by the value obtained.

These are arguments about the interpretation of data, not about the construction of data. A user may decide after the data are constructed that because they are inconsistent, irresponsible, and so on, he is not interested in them. They cease to be relevant for him and consequently are not valid for his purposes. But if they were constructed according to the wishes of the original client and are judged to have been accurate in the accounts they gave of the social world at the time they were constructed, they are valid for that client.

The main problem with opinion data – a problem, still, of inter-pretation, not of construction – stems from the fact that it is the present state of a potentially continually changing process that is measured when an opinion statement is obtained. A survey is a knowledge-production enterprise for a client and a researcher – their knowledge, they hope, will increase with each knowledge-production task the informant performs. It must also be a knowledge-production exercise for the informant. I have said already that an act of measurement asserts more about the social world than it asks. Its assertion is directed at the informant. Undoubtedly, taking part in a survey is a learning experience for the informant. His schemata, therefore, must undergo some change during the survey; and it is quite possible that the schemata that underlie the opinions he is asked to express during the survey change while the survey is happening. It may be something to do with his initial encounter with the survey; it may be the earlier questions and preambles to questions; it may be new thoughts sparked off within the informant while answering earlier questions; or it may be the opinion question itself. Any, or all, of these could produce changes in the schemata that direct the person's statements of opinion. With opinion questions phrased in the present tense, therefore, we confront the same fundamental issue as with a record-keeping survey – the possibility that the social world measured in the survey may have been altered by the survey itself.

8

Afterword: The Approach to Measurement Error

A failure of data construction in social surveys can reveal itself in one of two ways: either as a non-datum, an outcome irrelevant to the needs of the survey client, or as an invalid datum, a knowledge product which in a formal sense meets the client's needs but fails to provide an accurate reflection of the state of the social world. Two opposing approaches to failures of data construction may be discerned. In this chapter these two approaches to measurement error and the very different orientations to the whole data-construction process that underlie them are presented and compared.

(1) With the approach advocated in this book the focus is upon the individual datum. We cannot validate at datum level but we can set out with the intention of achieving a good datum for every separate act of measurement. We regard error as preventable; or, if it cannot be prevented, as curable so long as it is caught immediately after it has been committed. It is not a sort of original sin that must be atoned for in our data-construction procedures. Rather, error is seen as a fault introduced from without; the researcher who fails to construct a good datum bungles, and his bungle is capable of being avoided. The notion is that, since people can and do know the social world and can and do communicate their knowledge of it to others, if we fail to form a good datum about the social world in a social survey it must be that either we failed to satisfy the conditions on the design of a data matrix expounded in Chapter 5 or we failed to satisfy the conditions on good task performance by the informant or the researcher-as-classifier described in Chapters 6 and 7.

Errors are preventable because they can be foreseen. The process validation of data can be carried out in advance of a survey just as successfully as it can be carried out after a survey. Since procedures must be specified before they are put into effect (without such prior specification there is no chance of achieving a standard treatment down the columns of the data matrix), the comparison of procedures with theoretical requirements can be made as soon as the procedures are specified and before they are put into effect. This is what happens when a pre-pilot test is made of the design of a data matrix or when a pilot test is made of the mode of measurement for a survey variate.

Those errors that are not prevented may be corrected immediately after they occur, averting any damage to data quality. All this calls for is a natural human self-awareness – a monitoring of one's own task performance. Thus an interviewer who spots her own slip in asking a question or recording an answer should be able to put the matter right; an informant who has been persuaded to take his work as an informant seriously is likely of his own accord to detect and correct an error in his own answer; and an office coder who goes about his task carefully should notice if, say, he fails to enter a code where one is required. All these are instances of self-editing, and their effect upon data quality is just the same as the interventions by the interviewer in an act of measurement to manipulate the conditions for good work by an informant or the checks upon an office coder made by his coding supervisor.

By these actions (taken either in advance of, or immediately after, the commission of an error) the researcher should be able to safeguard or to restore the validity of each datum. There will, no doubt, always be some errors that slip through none the less but these should be few enough not to jeopardise the interpretation of the data. The responsible researcher's aim, with this approach, is to reveal these errors – a part of his larger aim of making the data of the survey transparent. The most conspicuous errors are the non-data, and no attempt will be made to dress these up as data after the event when it is too late to set them right. Much less conspicuous are the invalid data, relevant but inaccurate, and here the researcher will strive to ensure that these are constructed according to rules made public as part of the survey classification scheme and not according to the private whim of the informant or field coder or office coder.

(2) The alternative approach focuses not upon the individual datum but upon data at large. It sweeps away the problem of inaccuracy by assuming that invalidity at datum level will cancel out when cases are treated in the aggregate. And instead of forestalling error it seeks to treat with it after the event, at the final stage of data construction. At this stage various edit checks are instituted, as was described in Chapter 3, and non-data are replaced with 'imputed' data. But, unlike the self-editing carried out immediately after an error has been made that can rectify the datum, this editing occurs too late to be able – except in a very few cases – to restore accuracy to an inaccurate datum. The choice, then, is between prevention or cure of error, on the one hand, and a tidying-up cosmetic operation, a sweeping under the carpet, or – to pursue the medical analogy – a disposing of the body on the other. And since the only form of validation this approach employs is comparison of data with standard

values, and standard values are usually either impossible or impracticable to obtain, the consequences of making the cancelling-out assumptions and the post-survey imputations cannot be investigated.

The cancelling-out assumption seems sometimes to lie behind the recommendation frequently made that a battery of opinion questions should be asked rather than a single question. Of course, if the opinion is multi-faceted and each facet would be represented by a different survey variate, then clearly a separate mode of measurement must be devised for each facet. But if the opinion is single-faceted and each question represents a separate attempt at the measurement of the same variate, there is no guarantee that several questions in combination will do better than one question on its own. A single mode of measurement that satisfies the conditions for good data construction would offer a better chance of success than several that fail to satisfy these conditions – as well as imposing less burden on informants and being less prodigal of research time.

The cancelling-out assumption seems also to lie behind a suggestion often made for reducing response variance in interview surveys. It is well established that response variance tends to increase (1) the more an interviewer makes the same kind of error repeatedly and (2) the greater the number of interviews allocated to each interviewer. One way of coping is to reduce the number of interviews per interviewer. Fellegi and Sunter report that this was taken to its ultimate conclusion in the 1971 Canadian Census in which the decision was made that 'every sampling unit would become its own interviewer': 'face-to-face enumeration' was replaced with 'self-enumeration' (1973: 7–8). This decision, of course, is based on the assumption that different interviewers will make different types of error. (If interviewer assignments in a survey were halved and the number of interviewers was doubled but each pair of interviewers made the same type of error, clearly the response variance would not be reduced.) In fact, it seems likely that the common training given to interviewers in the same field force would encourage contagion of errors within that force. A better solution might be to tackle the problem of interviewer error at source. If an interviewer is making the same type of field coding error repeatedly it may be that she has failed to understand the coding frame. Perhaps the coding task is too complex for a field coder and should be assigned to an office coder. Certainly it would seem that one or more of the conditions for good data construction is not being satisfied.

Imputation means the insertion of a value into a data matrix cell based on something other than knowledge of the part of the social world defined by that cell – that is, knowledge of the position taken by *that* case on *that* variate at the moment of measurement. In a survey this knowledge can only be provided by the informant, but by the post-survey editing stage it is too late to ask the informant. Imputation, therefore, removes the INFORMANT from the survey data model, CLIENT – RESEARCHER – INFORMANT – SOCIAL WORLD. And since the informant is the only link between the researcher and the social world when survey data proper are being constructed, removal of the INFORMANT means also removal of the SOCIAL WORLD from the model. Knowledge of the world is now being based not on an interaction of Subject (knower) and Object (thing-to-be-known) but on the Subject alone.

The imputed value in a given survey may be arrived at without taking account of other data of that survey – for instance, by some chance event such as the spin of a coin. Often, however, it is arrived at from a scrutiny of other values in the data matrix of that survey. An empty cell, for example, may be filled by copying the value from the equivalent cell for a case that shows an identical profile of values on several other variates. But in the interpretation of data each datum is regarded as a separate item of evidence arrived at independently of every other one. Imputation, therefore, contradicts basic assumptions of both data construction and data interpretation. In the last analysis, if imputation is a legitimate procedure then no survey needed to be done. And conversely, if a survey does need to be done, imputation cannot be legitimate.

The two approaches to measurement error portrayed in this chapter represent opposite ends of a continuum. The practical researcher, dogged by time and budget pressures and with an insistent client yapping at his heels, cannot always take the purist position advocated here but, if his work is to be of value to social science, must avoid taking a casual attitude to measurement error. Data quality depends greatly upon the contributions to data construction made by the interviewers, the office coding unit and the informants. If measurement error is accepted on the grounds that it is unavoidable, is not really damaging anyway and can be disguised, this attitude will soon communicate itself to the survey organisation's staff. Willingness on the part of the researcher-as-classifier to do the hard work required is one of the prior conditions for good data construction but can only be sustained if the organisation distinguishes a good datum from a bad, a good act of measurement from a poor one. Poor work by the research director will not go unnoticed by the informant. How can we demand that he should work hard in performing a task if it is evident to him that the task he is set was sloppily designed? Good social science requires good surveys, and good surveys are founded on good data.

References and Author Index

The numbers following each entry refer to the page numbers in the book where this item is referred to.

American Marketing Association (1937) *The Technique of Marketing Research* (New York: McGraw-Hill). **53**

Baddeley, A. (1981) 'The cognitive psychology of everyday life', *British Journal of Psychology*, vol. 72, pp. 257–69. **75**

Bailar, B. A. and Lanphier, C. M. (1978) *Development of Survey Methods to Assess Survey Practices* (Washington, DC: American Statistical Association). **44–5**

Bainbridge, S., Dodd, P., Eldridge, J. and Lewis, D. (1979) 'Heights and weights feasibility study', *Survey Methodology Bulletin*, no. 7, pp. 8–12. **16**

Barton, A. H. (1958) 'Asking the embarrassing question', *Public Opinion Quarterly*, vol. 22, pp. 67–8. **113**

Belson, W. A. (1981) *The Design and Understanding of Survey Questions* (Aldershot, Hants: Gower). **55**

Berelson, B. (1954) 'Content analysis', in *Handbook of Social Psychology*, Vol. 1, ed. G. Lindzey (Reading, Mass.: Addison-Wesley), pp. 488–522. **6**

Bernal, J. D. (1965) *Science in History*, Vol. 2, 3rd edn (Harmondsworth, Middx: Penguin). **28**

Bingham, W. V. D. and Moore, B. V. (1959) *How to Interview*, 4th revised edn (New York: Harper). **115**

Blalock, H. M. (1968) 'The measurement problem: a gap between the languages of theory and research', in *Methodology in Social Research*, ed. H. and A. Blalock (New York: McGraw-Hill), pp. 5–27. **24**

Bott, M. F. (1970) 'Computational linguistics', in *New Horizons in Linguistics*, ed. J. Lyons (Harmondsworth, Middx.: Penguin), pp. 215–28. **124**

Bradburn, N. M. and Sudman, S., with the assistance of Blair, E., Locander, W., Miles, C., Singer, E. and Stocking, C. (1979) *Improving Interview Method and Questionnaire Design* (San Francisco; New York: Jossey-Bass). **34, 37, 55, 62, 106**

Bulmer, M. (1979) 'Concepts in the analysis of qualitative data', *Sociological Review*, vol. 27, pp. 651–77. **76**

Cahalan, D. (1968) 'Correlates of respondent accuracy in the Denver validity survey', *Public Opinion Quarterly*, vol. 32, pp. 607–21. **34**

Campbell, D. T. (1954) 'The informant in quantitative research', *American Journal of Sociology*, vol. 60, pp. 339–42. **19**

Campbell, D. T. and Fiske, D. W. (1959) 'Convergent and discriminant validation by the multitrait-multimethod matrix', *Psychological Bulletin*, vol. 56, pp. 81–105. **19**

Campbell, D. T. and Stanley, J. C. (1963) 'Experimental and quasi-experimental designs for research', in *Handbook of Research on Teaching*, ed. N. L. Gage (Chicago: Rand McNally), pp. 171–246. **56**

Cannell, C. F. and Kahn, R. L. (1953) 'The collection of data by interviewing', in *Research Methods in the Behavioral Sciences*, ed. L. Festinger and D. Katz (New York: Dryden), pp. 327–80. **55**

Cannell, C. F. and Kahn, R. L. (1968) 'Interviewing', in *Handbook of Social Psychology*, Vol. 2, ed. G. Lindzey and E. Aronson, 2nd edn (Reading, Mass.: Addison-Wesley), pp. 526–95. **6, 13, 34, 39, 55**

Cannell, C. F., Lawson, S. A. and Hausser, D. L. (1975) *A Technique for Evaluating Interviewer Performance* (Ann Arbor, Mich.: Survey Research Center). **123**

Cannell, C. F., Marquis, K. H. and Laurent, A. (1977) *A Summary of Studies of Interviewing Methodology*, Vital and Health Statistics, Series 2, No. 69 (Rockville, Md: National Center for Health Statistics). **34, 55, 61**

Cannell, C. F., Oksenberg, L. and Converse, J. M. (eds) (1979) *Experiments in Interviewing Techniques* (Ann Arbor, Mich.: Survey Research Center). **55, 103, 115**

Cartwright, D. (1978) 'Theory and practice', *Journal of Social Issues*, vol. 34, pp. 168–80. **xii**

Cicourel, A. V. (1964) *Method and Measurement in Sociology* (New York: The Free Press). **126**

Cochran, W. (1953) *Sampling Techniques* (New York: Wiley). **52**

Coombs, C. H. (1953) 'Theory and methods of social measurement', in *Research Methods in the Behavioral Sciences*, ed. L. Festinger and D. Katz (New York: Dryden), pp. 471–535. **5, 90**

Coombs, C. H. (1964) *A Theory of Data* (New York: Wiley). **xi, 5**

Cronbach, L. J. and Meehl, P. E. (1955) 'Construct validity in psychological tests', *Psychological Bulletin*, vol. 52, pp. 281–301. **36**

Davis, J. A. (1971) *Elementary Survey Analysis* (Englewood Cliffs, NJ: Prentice-Hall). **6, 9**

Deming, W. E. (1944) 'On errors in surveys', *American Sociological Review*, vol. 9, pp. 359–69. **40, 52**

Department of Employment (1972) *Classification of Occupations and Directory of Occupational Titles* [CODOT], Vols 1–3 (London: HMSO). **84**

Fellegi, I. P. and Sunter, A. B. (1973) 'Balance between different sources of survey errors – some Canadian experiences', *Proceedings of the 39th Session of the International Statistical Institute*, Vol. 3 (Vienna: Österreichisches Statistisches Zentralamt), pp. 334–55. **37, 137**

Field, M. D. (1979) 'Polls and public policy', *Journal of Advertising Research*, vol. 19, pp. 11–17. **4, 41**

Fothergill, J. E. and Willcock, H. D. (1953) 'Interviewers and interviewing', *The Incorporated Statistician*, supplement to vol. 5, no. 4, pp. 37–56. **55**

Galtung, J. (1967) *Theory and Methods of Social Research* (London: Allen & Unwin). **xi, 13, 21, 25, 55, 130**

General Register Office (1863) *Census of England and Wales, 1861. Vol. III: General Report* (London: HMSO). **84–5**

Glass, G. V. (1976) 'Primary, secondary, and meta-analysis of research', *Educational Researcher*, vol. 6, pp. 3–8. **28**

Glenn, N. (1978) 'The General Social Surveys: editorial introduction to a symposium', *Contemporary Sociology*, vol. 7, pp. 532–4. **28**

Glock, C. Y. (1967) 'Survey design and analysis in sociology', in *Survey Research in the Social Sciences*, ed. C. Y. Glock (New York: Russell Sage Foundation). **18**

Gray, P. G. (1956) 'Examples of interviewer variability taken from two sample surveys', *Applied Statistics*, vol. 5, pp. 73–85. **55**

Hakim, C. (1982) *Secondary Analysis in Social Research* (London: Allen & Unwin). **28**

Hedges, B. (1982) in 'Discussion of the paper by Dr Kalton and Dr Schuman', *Journal of the Royal Statistical Association*, ser. A, vol. 145, pp. 57–73. See Kalton and Schuman (1982). **47**

Hempel, C. G. (1952) *Fundamentals of Concept Formation in Empirical Science* (Chicago: University of Chicago Press). **126**

Henson, R., Cannell, C. F. and Lawson, S. (1977) 'An experiment in interviewer style and questionnaire form', in *Experiments in Interviewing Technique*, ed. C. F. Cannell, L. Oksenberg and J. M. Converse (Ann Arbor, Mich.: Survey Research Center), pp. 21–44. **62**

Heyns, R. W. and Lippitt, R. (1954) 'Systematic observational techniques', in *Handbook of Social Psychology*, Vol. 1, ed. G. Lindzey. (Reading, Mass.: Addison-Wesley), pp. 370–404. **16**

Hitlin, R. (1976) 'On question wording and stability of response', *Social Science Research*, vol. 5, pp. 39–41. **57–9**

Hiż, H. (ed.) (1978) *Questions* (Dordrecht: Reidel). **97**

Huxley, T. H. (1893) *Method and Results* (London: Macmillan). **4**

Hyman, H. H. (1944) 'Do they tell the truth?', *Public Opinion Quarterly*, vol. 8, pp. 557–9. **114**

Hyman, H.H. *et al.* (1954) *Interviewing in Social Research* (Chicago: University of Chicago Press). **55**

Jespersen, O. (1933) *Essentials of English Grammar* (New York: Holt, Rinehart & Winston). **97–8**

Kahn, R. L. and Cannell, C. F. (1957) *The Dynamics of Interviewing* (New York: Wiley). **55**

Kalton, G. and Schuman, H. (1982) 'The effect of the question on survey responses', *Journal of the Royal Statistical Society*, ser. A, vol. 145, pp. 42–57. **33, 38, 55**

Kalton, G. and Stowell, R. (1979) 'A study of coder variability', *Applied Statistics*, vol. 28, pp. 276–89. **55, 117, 129**

Kaplan, A. (1964) *The Conduct of Inquiry* (New York: Chandler). **76**

Kemsley, W. (1979) 'Collecting data on economic flow variables using interviews and record keeping', in *The Recall Method in Social Surveys*, ed. L. Moss and H. Goldstein (London: University of London Institute of Education), pp. 115–33. **31**

Kendall, P. and Lazarsfeld, P. F. (1950) 'Problems of survey analysis', in *Continuities in Social Research: Studies in the Scope and Method of 'The American Soldier'*, ed. R. K. Merton and P. F. Lazarsfeld (New York: The Free Press), pp. 133–96. **62**

Klatzky, R. L. (1980) *Human Memory: Structures and Processes*, 2nd edn (San Francisco: Freeman). **110**

Koomen, W. and Dijkstra, W. (1975) 'Effects of question length on verbal behavior in a bias-reduced interview situation', *European Journal of Social Psychology*, vol. 5, pp. 399–403. **60–1**

Kruskal, W. (1981) 'Statistics in society: problems unsolved and unformulated', *Journal of the American Statistical Association*, vol. 76, pp. 505–15. **37**

Laurent, A. (1972) 'Effects of question length on reporting behavior in the survey interview', *Journal of the American Statistical Association*, vol. 67, pp. 298–305. **61**

Lazarsfeld, P. F. (1935) 'The art of asking why', *National Marketing Review*, vol. 1, pp. 26–38. **110**

Lazarsfeld, P. F. (1970) 'Sociology', in *Main Trends of Research in the Social and Human Sciences* (Paris and The Hague: Mouton/UNESCO), pp. 61–165. **25**

Lazarsfeld, P. F., Pasanella, A. and Rosenberg, M. (eds) (1972) *Continuities in the Language of Social Research* (New York: The Free Press). **8, 25**

Lazarsfeld, P. F. and Rosenberg, M. (eds) (1955) *The Language of Social Research* (Glencoe, Ill.: The Free Press). **8, 25, 51, 62**

Leech, G. (1974) *Semantics* (Harmondsworth, Middx.: Penguin). **18**

Lewin, K. (1951) *Field Theory in Social Science*, ed. D. Cartwright (New York: Harper). **11, 14, 52**

Lyons, J. (1970) 'Introduction', in *New Horizons in Linguistics*, ed. J. Lyons (Harmondsworth, Middx.: Penguin), pp. 7–28. **105**

Maccoby, E. E. and Maccoby, N. (1954) 'The interview: a tool of social science', in *Handbook of Social Psychology*, Vol. 1, ed. G. Lindzey (Reading, Mass.: Addison-Wesley), pp. 449–87. **55**

Madge, J. (1953) *The Tools of Social Science* (London: Longman). **16**

Marsh, C. (1982) *The Survey Method* (London: Allen & Unwin). **4, 49**

Matarazzo, J. D., Wiens, A. N., Saslow, G., Dunham, R. M. and Voas, R. B. (1964) 'Speech durations of astronaut and ground communicator', *Science*, vol. 143, pp. 148–50. **60**

Matarazzo, J. D. and Wiens, A. N. (1972) *The Interview: Research on its Anatomy and Structure* (Chicago: Aldine-Atherton). **60**

Mellone, S. H. (1945) *Elements of Modern Logic*, 2nd edn (London: University Tutorial Press). **120**

Miller, G. A. (1978) 'Practical and lexical knowledge', in *Cognition and Categorization*, ed. E. Rosch and B. B. Lloyd (Hillsdale, NJ: Lawrence Erlbaum), pp. 305–19. **124**

Minton, G. (1969) 'Inspection and correction error in data processing', *Journal of the American Statistical Association*, vol. 64, pp. 1256–75. **55**

Mischel, W. (1979) 'On the interface of cognition and personality', *American Psychologist*, vol. 34, pp. 740–54. **112**

Moser, C. A. and Kalton, G. (1971) *Survey Methods in Social Investigation*, 2nd edn (London: Heinemann). **56**

Moss, L. and Goldstein, H. (eds) (1979) *The Recall Method in Social Surveys* (London: University of London Institute of Education). **109**

Myers, R. J. (1954) 'Accuracy of age reporting in the 1950 United States Census', *Journal of the American Statistical Association*, vol. 49, pp. 826–31. **37**

Neisser, U. (1976) *Cognition and Reality* (San Francisco: Freeman). **10, 12–13, 89, 91**

Neter, J. and Waksberg, J. (1964) 'A study of response errors in expenditures data from household interviews', *Journal of the American Statistical Association*, vol. 59, pp. 18–55. **110**

Neurath, P. M. (1979) 'The writings of Paul F. Lazarsfeld: a topical bibliography', in *Qualitative and Quantitative Social Research*, ed. R. K. Merton, J. S. Coleman and P. H. Rossi (New York: The Free Press), pp. 365–87. **54**

Noelle, E. [later Noelle-Neumann, E.] (1962) *On the Methodological Progress in Survey Research* (Allensbach and Bonn: Verlag für Demoskopie). **41**

Noelle-Neumann, E. (1980) 'The public opinion research correspondent', *Public Opinion Quarterly*, vol. 44, pp. 585–97. **50**

Nunnally, J. C. (1967) *Psychometric Theory* (New York: McGraw-Hill). **33, 40, 48**

Oksenberg, L. (1978) 'New interviewing techniques designed to improve validity of response', *Proceedings of the 1978 American Statistical Association* (Washington, DC), pp. 49–52. **103**

OPCS (1970) *Classification of Occupations 1970* (London: HMSO). **80, 83, 123, 126**

OPCS (1980) *Classification of Occupations and Coding Index 1980* (London: HMSO). **76**

Parry, H. J. and Crossley, H. M. (1950) 'Validity of responses to survey questions', *Public Opinion Quarterly*, vol. 14, pp. 61–80. **34**

Payne, S. L. (1951, repr. 1980) *The Art of Asking Questions* (Princeton, NJ: Princeton University Press). **52, 59–60, 107**

Pettigrew, T. F. (1958) 'The measurement and correlates of category width as a cognitive variable', *Journal of Personality*, vol. 26, pp. 532–44. **123**

Plato (1973 edn) *Phaedrus and the Seventh and Eighth Letters*, trans. W. Hamilton (Harmondsworth, Middx: Penguin). **88–9**

Platt, J. (1972) 'Survey data and social policy', *British Journal of Sociology*, vol. 23, pp. 77–92. **3**

Quirk, R. (1976) *The Formal and Semantic Properties of Questions in Spoken English*, SSRC Final Report, HR2767. **97–8**

Ray, M. L. and Webb, E. J. (1966) 'Speech duration effects in the Kennedy news conferences', *Science*, vol. 153, pp. 899–901. **60**

Richardson, S. A., Dohrenwend, B. S. and Klein, D. (1965) *Interviewing: Its Forms and Functions* (New York: Basic Books). **6**

Rosch, E. (1978) 'Principles of categorization', in *Cognition and Categorization*, ed. E. Rosch and B. B. Lloyd (Hillsdale, NJ: Lawrence Erlbaum), pp. 27–48. **111–12, 131–32**

Rothman, J. (1980) 'Acceptance checks for ensuring quality in research', *Journal of the Market Research Society*, vol. 22, pp. 192–204. **41**

Saussure, F. de (1916; English trans. 1974) *Course in General Linguistics*, trans. W. Baskin (London: Fontana/Collins). **105**

Schuman, H. and Presser, S. (1978) 'Question wording as an independent variable in survey analysis', in *Survey Design and Analysis*, ed. D. F. Alwin (Beverly Hills, Calif.: Sage), pp. 27–46. **53**

Schuman, H. and Presser, S. (1979) 'The open and closed question', *American Sociological Review*, vol. 44, pp. 692–712. **92**

Schuman, H. and Presser, S. (1981) *Questions and Answers in Attitude Surveys* (New York: Academic Press). **55**

Stebbing, L. S. (1952) *A Modern Elementary Logic*, rev. C. W. K. Mundle (London: Methuen). **120**

Stouffer, S. A. *et al.* (1949/50) *Studies in Social Psychology in World War II*, Vols 1–4 (Princeton, NJ: Princeton University Press). **53**

Sudman, S. (1980) 'Reducing response error in surveys', *The Statistician*, vol. 29, pp. 237–73. **109–10**

Sudman, S. and Bradburn, N. M. (1974) *Response Effects in Surveys*

(Chicago: Aldine). **8, 28, 33, 109**

Tanenbaum, E. and Taylor, M. (undated) 'Data banks and theory confirmation: a review and a proposal', unpublished paper of the SSRC Survey Archive, University of Essex, Colchester, Essex. **64**

Tauber, E. M. (1981) 'The new JAR', *Journal of Advertising Research*, vol. 21, pp. 11–12. **64**

Todd, J. E., Walker, A. M. and Dodd, P. (1982) *Adult Dental Health, United Kingdom 1978*, Vol. 2 (London: HMSO). **16**

Torgerson, W. S. (1958) *Theory and Methods of Scaling* (New York: Wiley). **xi, 126**

Ullmann, S. (1962) *Semantics: An Introduction to the Science of Meaning* (Oxford: Blackwell). **111**

Ullmann, S. (1963) 'Semantic universals', in *Universals of Language*, ed. J. H. Greenberg (Cambridge, Mass.: MIT), pp. 172–207. **106**

US Bureau of the Census (1978) *An Evaluation of 1970 Census Occupational Classification*, Bureau of the Census Technical Paper No. 41. **85**

Walker, A. (1979) 'The measurement of distance travelled on foot in the "Pedestrian Habits" survey', *Survey Methodology Bulletin*, no. 8, pp. 16–20. **16**

Warner, S. L. (1965) 'Randomized response: a survey technique for eliminating evasive answer bias', *Journal of the American Statistical Association*, vol. 60, pp. 63–9. **113**

Webb, E. J., Campbell, D. T., Schwartz, R. D. and Sechrest, L. (1966) *Unobtrusive Measures: Non-reactive Research in the Social Sciences* (Chicago: Rand McNally).

Weber, M. (1949) *The Methodology of the Social Sciences*, trans. and ed. E. A. Shils and H. A. Finch (New York: The Free Press). **51**

Weick, K. E. (1968) 'Systematic Observational Methods', in *Handbook of Social Psychology*, Vol. 2, ed. G. Lindzey and E. Aronson, 2nd edn (Reading, Mass.: Addison-Wesley), pp. 357–451. **16**

Wells, A. F. (1935) *The Local Social Survey in Great Britain* (London: Allen & Unwin). **3**

Wimer, S. and Kelley, H. H. (1982) 'An investigation of the dimensions of causal attribution', *Journal of Personality and Social Psychology*, vol. 43, pp. 1142–62. **110**

Woodward, J. (1952) review of *The Art of Asking Questions* by S. L. Payne, *Public Opinion Quarterly*, vol. 16, pp. 138–9. **53**

Wyner, G. A. (1980) 'Response errors in self-reported number of arrests', *Sociological Methods and Research*, vol. 9, pp. 161–77. **38**

Zeisel, H. (1947) *Say It with Figures* (New York: Harper). **62**

Subject Index

(Includes names where not attached to references. Names attached to references are listed in the Author Index.)

ALLT- ʻR- YN LIBRARY